C. P. SNOW

C. P. SNOW

by Jerome Thale

New York

CHARLES SCRIBNER'S SONS

ACKNOWLEDGMENTS

For permission to quote from the works of C. P. Snow, acknowledgment is due to Charles Scribner's Sons.

Acknowledgments are also due to *Kenyon Review* and Sir Charles Snow (C. P. Snow, "Science, Politics and the Novelist"); *New Statesman* (Helen Gardner, "The World of C. P. Snow"); and *The Texas Quarterly* (Robert Greacen, "The World of C. P. Snow").

I wish especially to thank Marquette University for generously granting me a leave of absence to work on this book.

J. T.

✑ CONTENTS

ABBREVIATED TITLES USED IN REFERENCES

In all references to the novels of the "Strangers and Brothers" sequence, the first of the two page references given is to the English edition, the second (in parentheses) to the American edition, listed in the Bibliography (below, pp. 154) as standard.

A.	=	*The Affair.*
C.R.	=	*The Conscience of the Rich.*
H.	=	*Homecomings.*
L. & D.	=	*The Light and the Dark.*
M.	=	*The Masters.*
N.M.	=	*The New Men.*
S. & B.	=	*Strangers and Brothers.*
T.H.	=	*Time of Hope.*
C.P.	=	*Corridors of Power*

C. P. SNOW

1 ॐ

Life and Early Works

It is possible that C. P. Snow's life has at its center one of those dramas in which the hero, faced with a choice of ways, comes to decisive knowledge of himself. Having earned a Ph.D. in physics at twenty-five, done a good deal of research, and become a fellow of Christ's College, Snow did indeed give up a career as a scientist for one as a novelist. The transition, however, was gradual, and Snow's statements on the matter hardly suggest a dramatic movement of decision: "I knew my own ultimate vocation from the time I was about eighteen," but "I made my way in the most practicable career open to me, as a professional scientist." [1]

In any case Snow's subsequent career is, from a dramatic point of view, even less promising. It is largely a record of steady and unspectacular successes bringing Snow to his current eminence as a major novelist and as prophet with honor. The development of his art and thought is also undramatic. His basic ideas have remained remarkably consistent throughout the past thirty years, and his skill as a novelist has increased steadily rather than through any radical change in the nature of his art.

Nor does Snow's life fall into any of the recognizable categories for the writer—solitude, eccentricity, flamboyance. He seems simply to have lived his own interesting and varied life; he has no personal legend which can be easily popularized. There is, particularly in the years since his statements on science, government, and the two cultures, the picture of Snow as triple-threat man— scientist, novelist, administrator—but this is a legend of public record, not a personal one. With fame Snow has not become a "personality" but something like an institution, a pantocratic sage. None of this, however, has a great deal to do with the large agreeable man who doesn't particularly look like a novelist, an administrator, or a scientist, certainly not like a sage. Nor does it tell us a great deal about the creator of the "Strangers and Brothers" sequence.

The man who has written the "Strangers and Brothers" sequence does not talk much about himself, his friends do not gossip about him in print, and his activities get into the newspapers only when he gives a speech or receives an award—which he has done with great frequency since the late fifties. What one discovers about Snow is not anecdote and rumor, but a record of jobs held, novels written, and so on, the public record of a successful man.

Although he was born in 1905—that is, within the same ten-year span as Hemingway, Faulkner, Waugh, Auden—he belongs in terms of literary reputation to the post-war era. This is not just an accident of publication dates. At a time when Hemingway and Huxley, for example, have become classics fated to prescribed deference, it is possible for people to get excited praising or denouncing Snow: they become enthusiastic over him as a novelist who has something important to say to us, or feel indignant that he is promulgating dangerous attitudes that need to be denounced.

Thus, though Snow started writing as early as 1932 and published *The Search* in 1934, he seems to us to belong not with Lawrence, Kafka, Steinbeck, but with Bellow, Golding, Styron, Amis. And perhaps the largest reason for this is that the matters and attitudes which he has been writing about for thirty years have in the nineteen-fifties and -sixties become central in our thinking. Whether Snow is right or wrong, we recognize that he is talking about the things that concern us.

Snow was born in Leicester in 1905, the second of four sons. About his early life he has not said much. Parts of the childhood sections of *Time of Hope* appear to be autobiographical: the provincial town, the lower middle-class family, the father who is not very successful. Snow's grandfather had been a foreman in the Leicester Tramways department. His father was a clerk in a shoe-factory and played the organ in church (just as Lewis Eliot's father was a devoted member of a choral group). At Alderman Newton's school, Snow specialized in science, and later he worked as a laboratory assistant at the school while studying for a university scholarship. At Leicester University College he took a First Class Honours degree in chemistry in 1927. Snow recalls that at Leicester he drank a lot of beer and on one occasion wore a top hat around the town for a month to win a bet.[2] He received an M.Sc. from Leicester and was awarded a scholarship which enabled him to become a research student at Cambridge. In 1930 he received his Ph.D. and was elected a fellow of Christ's College.

He became a scientist, he says, because it was the only thing for a poor boy to do. But all along he had other ambitions and knew his "ultimate vocation" as a writer before he was twenty.[3] Still, like the hero of his novel *The Search,* he worked hard at science. Between 1929 and 1935 he published a good number of scientific papers, particularly on infra-red investigation of molecular structures. (One finds Snow on "The Overtone of Nitric Oxide" side by side with Dirac on "A Theory of Electrons and Protons" in *Royal Society Proceedings.*) [4]

About this time Snow began writing on scientific subjects for a general audience, particularly in *The Spectator:* "The Enjoyment of Science," "Science of the Year," "What We Need from Applied Science" (a forecast of *The Two Cultures* twenty-five years later), "Rejuvenation Promises an End of Old Age." One of the earliest pieces, "Science of the Year," suggests something

of the later Snow and tells us a good deal about the
effect of his scientific *milieu:*

> There has never been such a time . . . [we are] lucky
> to be alive and lookers-on. . . . The spectacle of the
> world becomes more hopeless. But science moves from
> strength to strength.[5]

At Cambridge Snow figured for many undergraduates
as "the great emancipator" (one thinks of George Passant in *Strangers and Brothers*). We are told by S. Gorley Putt, who was a student at the time:

> His talk, without the slightest trace of donnish moder-
> ation, sprayed over life, love, politics, Proust. . . . It
> was all, at times, like a Verdurin party. . . .
>
> The very carelessness of Snow's approach was salu-
> tary to us, in those days. It mattered less, to our per-
> sonal growth, that Snow spoke rudely of *The Book of
> Kells,* than that he should have scattered his own
> books and papers all over the floor, should talk away
> into the night while playing like a kitten with a ping-
> pong ball, or even that he should show an Olympian
> ineptitude for the simple business of keeping his coal
> fire alight.[6]

Gregariousness and a steady output of research did
not keep Snow from the writing of fiction. In 1932 he
published a detective story, *Death under Sail,* which was
fairly well received (it was a Crime Club selection in
the United States). This did not get him very far
towards his real vocation, and, as he said somewhat rue-
fully many years later, detective stories "are great fun to
write, but they take almost as long as a novel proper." [7]

Snow's next venture was less happy, a work in the Wells tradition of science fiction about a society that has developed a process for rejuvenation. The book, *New Lives for Old*, was published anonymously and was not very successful.

The next turn in Snow's career was the one that forced a decision between science and literature. As his friend William Cooper says:

> Snow's turning-point, a piece of research that went wrong through oversight, was externally rather like that in Arthur Miles's scientific career [in *The Search*]. . . . From then on he did no more research.[8]

The Search is in many ways a conventional novel, but it suggests a number of Snow's later concerns and key ideas.

In 1935 Snow became Tutor at Christ's, his first involvement in administration. In 1938 he published a brief and somewhat awkward pamphlet on Richard Aldington; the same year he became editor of *Discovery*, a popular scientific periodical, and also of the Cambridge Library of Modern Science.

Snow's movement away from science went at this point not so much towards literature as towards administration. There was first of all the Tutorship at Christ's; then in 1939 he was appointed to a Royal Society committee on the use of scientific personnel. After that he became a full-time administrator:

> It happened through the flukes of war—including meeting W. L. Bragg in the buffet on Kettering sta-

tion on a very cold morning in 1939, which had a determining influence on my practical life.[9]

For a time he was an assistant to Lord Hankey, an administrator from whom, Snow says, he learned a great deal. This connection with government was the beginning of a career as a civil servant, lasting nearly twenty years, for which he was made a C.B.E. in 1943 and knighted in 1957. During the War he was with the Ministry of Labour, where he was responsible for the allocation of scientific personnel, and after the War he was appointed consultant for the recruitment of scientists to government service. From 1945 to 1960 he served as a Civil Service Commissioner. In 1947, after serving as an adviser for three years, he became a member of the Board of Directors of the English Electric Company. With Labour's victory in 1964 Snow resumed his official connection with government—as Parliamentary Secretary for the Ministry of Technology and as Lord Snow, of Leicester. Life seemed to follow art with a surprising promptness: a month before the election Snow published *Corridors of Power,* whose hero is at first a Parliamentary Secretary. More interesting is the irony that Snow's latest distinction comes just when the "Strangers and Brothers" sequence is beginning to address itself to the theme of the renunciation of power.

Snow remained a bachelor until 1950, when he married Pamela Hansford Johnson, the novelist (who in 1944 had described Snow as "the only novelist of under forty years of age of whose future I am not in the slightest doubt").[10] They have one son, born in 1952, and live in London, though Snow has done a good deal of traveling. Since the War he has devoted more and more of his time to his ultimate career, the writing of fiction.

After the false starts of the detective story and the science fiction work, and the beginning made in *The Search,* Snow conceived the idea for the "Strangers and Brothers" sequence:

> I had the idea out of the blue—in what seemed like a single moment—in Marseilles on 1 January, 1935. I was walking down the Canebière. It was a bitterly cold night, well below freezing point. I was staying in Marseilles for the night, having flown down from London, and was off on a boat to Sicily the next day. I was extremely miserable. Everything, personal and creative, seemed to be going wrong. Suddenly I saw, or felt, or experienced, or whatever you like to call it, both the outline of the entire *Strangers and Brothers* sequence and its inner organisation, that is, the response or dialectic between Lewis Eliot as observer and as the focus of direct experience. As soon as this happened, I felt extraordinarily happy. I got the whole conception, I think, so far as that means anything, in a few minutes.[11]

The first volume, titled *Strangers and Brothers,* was published in 1940, the second, *The Light and the Dark,* in 1947, and since then seven more novels have appeared, roughly at two-year intervals.

During the nineteen-fifties, Snow became famous, first in a modest way as a novelist. Then, simultaneously, his reputation as a novelist became much greater and he became known as a commentator on public affairs—science and government, disarmament and peace, and education. As late as 1947 he was known to *The Times,* reporting on his election as a Director of the English Electric Company, as "Dr. C. Percy Snow." And as a student of reputations, Snow is perhaps amused by the fact that he was in Debrett before he was in most of the standard biographical guides to writers. An unusual distinction is that he was on the list that Himmler had prepared of people to be rounded up after a German occupation of Britain in 1940.[12] The record of his more conventional honors is impressive: lectureships at Cambridge and Harvard; numerous honorary degrees; election as Rector of St. Andrew's University. And, particularly since his lecture on *The Two Cultures* in 1959, he has done a good deal of lecturing and has been a visiting notable at American universities and a participant in symposia.

In recent years Snow probably has been better known as a sage than as a novelist, and his pronouncements on public questions have generated a fair amount of hostility. He has, however, wisely not engaged in controversy. Perhaps the best statement on Snow's current fame is Putt's:

> It is not difficult for his friends to detect in the present-day Sir Charles, the Rede Lecturer, those same qualities which in C. P. Snow the scientific research-worker might seem to have indicated a fixed temperamental opposition to the very kind of prestige he now enjoys. For "moral vanity" has always been, and still is, his favourite Aunt Sally at which to shy coconuts. He has never pretended that self-interest was a higher manifestation of moral philosophy, nor has he ever

held it a virtue to "do a man down", as he says, "in his own best interests". Even his enjoyment of fame, to those who know him well, remains one of his modest and disarming characteristics.[13]

Although Snow and his wife do not collaborate, they exchange ideas and criticism. Snow's appearance is a relaxed one, but his energy reminds one of the giants of the last century. At any given time he seems to have been involved in at least two careers. Nevertheless he finds writing slow and exhausting work and feels that he is lucky to turn out a thousand words a day. Many of his novels have been rewritten three times and end up quite unlike the first drafts. His ideal working day is from ten to two or three, interrupted by a cup of coffee. At present he has two volumes to publish in the "Strangers and Brothers" series, and beyond that—"Well, the plans for the future—to write all my time." [14] (This, of course, was said before his appointment as Parliamentary Secretary for the Ministry of Technology.)

Although Snow's early works are not particularly important in comparison with the "Strangers and Brothers" sequence, they are of some interest, both for themselves and in terms of his development. His first book, *Death under Sail* (1932), is a good example of the detective story of its time—when S. S. Van Dine was at the height of his popularity and Hercule Poirot still had his Hastings; and it is certainly readable today. Snow says of it in a prefatory "Author's Note" written for its reissue in 1959:

I was twenty-six when I wrote it; and to myself, though not to many others, it was a signal that I proposed to give up the scientific career [he continued to publish scientific articles for a few years after this] and take to writing novels. This had always been my intention; and now, I thought, it was about time to begin.

He continues that he is not sure why he started with a detective story: "I suspect I had a sense that I was one of those writers who have to nose their way among experience before they know what they are good for."

Snow's description of the work as "stylised, artificial . . . very much in the manner of the day," [15] is accurate enough; the *genre* is almost always stylized and was particularly so at that time.

Death under Sail, like all of Snow's fiction except *New Lives for Old,* is told by a narrator who is also a character in the story. He does not resemble the narrator of Snow's other fiction so much as the conventional foil in a detective story. He is an intentionally colorless character and is set off against the detective, who is essentially a reasoner and interpreter of motive. *Death under Sail* is a puzzle in which the detective reasons out, largely on psychological grounds, which of six people on a holiday cruise killed the host. The narrator and the detective are, in terms of the demands of the form, well characterized; the other characters are less satisfactory.

The relative lack of action, the general bareness of the style, and the emphasis on psychological analysis might give hints that Snow is the author, but on the whole the book is not distinctively Snow's. It does not give signs of the power and skill of the later novels. Snow seems, as he says, to have been finding his way, engaging in a good deal of analysis, but lightly and within a restricted set of conventions. And in fact the analysis is subordinated to the puzzle rather than offered as presentation of character for its own sake.

Death under Sail was not an especially promising beginning. In a later book the narrator reflects on what an absurd practice it would be if beginning writers were required (as scientists are) [16] to demonstrate competence in conventional and uninspired work, such as the detective story. Still, it places Snow in what is for poets at least an ancient and honorable tradition—the writer mastering a highly conventionalized form as a way of learning his craft.

Snow's second piece of fiction, *New Lives for Old* (1933), is, in its lack of sureness, rather more like a first novel than *Death under Sail*. It is neither an autobiographical nor a straight realistic novel—Snow was edging his way toward the conventional realistic novel and toward his own peculiar kind of fiction. Insofar as its plot depends on the discovery of a hormone which brings people in their sixties back to where they were in their thirties, *New Lives for Old* is science fiction. But beyond that there is none of the fantasy, allegory, or concern with technology that is usual in science fiction. Snow is interested in age and youth, in comfortable and discontented temperaments, and in the characters' second chance of fulfilment. And what he has to say about these subjects is said largely within a realistic framework.

After an initial section about the discovery and publication of the rejuvenation process (the government is

worried about increasing unemployment), the plot of
New Lives for Old focuses on the love affairs of two of
the rejuvenated: the one finds a fulfilment he had never
known before, the other loses his heart but cannot hold
the girl. In the final section set thirty years later, the
scientist who had opposed publication of the discovery
and now does not want to be rejuvenated discovers,
after the dangers of a revolution, that he would like to
go on living.

New Lives for Old is not a very good novel. Neither
the flesh-hating scientist nor the cynical writer is very
original or very convincing, and the heroine is at best
shadowy. The book has awkward shifts in focus and
point of view and a good deal of cliché and unsuccessful
rumination. Snow himself now describes it as a "very
bad book," and he published it anonymously in the first
instance, partly because of hesitation about its quality,
partly because he feared it would injure his scientific-
academic career. Its fundamental trouble seems to be
that Snow was not certain what kind of book he wanted
to write and did not have the artistic self-possession to
work through stereotypes to real characters.

Though *New Lives for Old* does not give much prom-
ise of the novelist that was to emerge later, it does have
interesting suggestions of ideas that Snow was to develop
later. Vanden, the discontented novelist, and Pilgrim,
the scientist at one with himself, perhaps suggest the
famous division of the two cultures (later, in the fiction,
Snow makes the discontented more complex and more
convincing and he looks more critically at the characters
who are at one with themselves). Already, too, we can

see Snow's interest in those who struggle with their natures, the high value he places on honesty with one's
self, and his awareness that even in the best of men
honesty is imperfect.

In the light of history and of Snow's later pronouncements there seems to be an allegorical import in *New
Lives for Old*. Rejuvenation seems a symbol of technical
and scientific progress generally—which, as Snow has
been saying for thirty years, has in fact lengthened life.
The social and political implications of rejuvenation
(which are not much developed in the novel) fore-
shadow Snow's later discussions of the rich and the
poor nations.

After these somewhat specialized ventures, Snow
wrote what may be for all practical purposes considered
his first novel, *The Search*, published in 1934. It is
much better written than his previous fiction, and better than most first novels. And it gives a good many
hints of the direction of Snow's development and the
nature of his later achievement. In fact it is almost a
preliminary sketch for the "Strangers and Brothers"
sequence.

The Search is the story of Arthur Miles, who like
Snow himself is a poor boy undertaking a career in science by means of scholarships and his own talent. We
see him on the rise as a promising researcher and learn
the story of his love for Audrey. When Audrey leaves
him, he devotes himself fully to science, looking forward
to the time when he can head a bio-physical institute.
Just as he is about to receive the appointment, he makes
an error in research that costs him the job and will set

him back years in his career. In the first part of the novel he had discovered that he really did not want to marry Audrey; in the second he discovers that he is not really interested in science. At the end he finds fulfilment in a second love and a new career as a writer.

On the surface there seems to be a conflict between science and love, but Arthur Miles' trouble is not excessive devotion to science or to a career but his inability to give himself either in love or in an unreserved "faith" in the pursuit of truth. His search, then, covers science, ambition, love. The connection between these is sometimes loose, and one of the novel's difficulties is that it has too much thematic material which is not satisfactorily brought together. Certainly one feels a shift from love as the dominant theme in the first part to desire for power in the second.

Although the hero's problem and general situation suggest much of the material of the Lewis Eliot novels (the abandonment of a career, inability to give himself, the two loves, and so on), the themes are not worked out with the penetration or artistic reach of *Time of Hope* and *Homecoming*. When Snow made use of these themes again, they became the substance for two books rather than one.

The Search is on the whole a conventional realistic novel. As such, it has a number of limitations: the themes are not precisely defined; the minor characters are generally weak; there is a good deal of talkiness, a lack of drama. At his best, Snow does well here what he does superlatively in his later novels: thus a section on a committee is good but superficial by comparison with similar sections in *The Light and the Dark* and *The Masters.*

Arthur Miles turns away from science because he lacks the faith that it demands and he must have something to which he can give himself completely. What brings him to writing is his increasing interest in "human intricacies" [17] and his discovery that the one thing which he finds interesting for its own sake is the study of people. Whatever Snow's motives, he, like Miles, turned away from science toward writing. But he had not yet discovered his own peculiar line of development. As he says in the "Author's Note" to *Death under Sail,* he was a slow developer and had to nose out his vocation through experience. By 1934 he had done a good deal of nosing and had completed his apprenticeship as a writer. His vocation was ahead in the "Strangers and Brothers" series.

2 ᘒ

Snow and the Liberal Context

WITH Snow, as with any contemporary or near-contemporary writer, we have to decide whether to look at him as part of the immediate scene or in the long view of literary history, whether to view him in the way we do Pasternak and Salinger or in the way we do Tolstoy and Jane Austen. Snow's current reputation is very much of the first kind, and his novels are part of the dialectic of the age. In a later chapter I shall say something about Snow's art and about what gives his novels a value beyond their immediate significance. But at the moment I am concerned with Snow as part of the contemporary scene, and specifically with the paradox that

Snow's ideas and attitudes look old-fashioned while at
the same time many readers find that he gives one of the
fullest and most significant accounts of the contemporary world.

Certainly Snow's liberal humanism is strangely un-
fashionable in an age which has gone through Marxism
and Freudianism and is now fascinated by orthodox the-
ology and existentialism. And it has been said that
Snow's writing is based on a hostility to most of what has
gone on in literature in the past thirty-five years and
that he has contributed nothing to the art of the novel.

Much of Snow's success and peculiar appeal can be
traced to the shift away from ideology, and, what is
closely related to it, the traditions of the twentieth-
century novel. In 1949 it was possible for Lionel Trilling to announce that our sole and dominant intellectual
tradition was the liberal one. But as that was uttered it
was ceasing to be true. The Cold War has negated the
old liberal pieties in international affairs (and liberals
almost as much as anybody have shifted emphasis from
morality to power). The achievement of much of the
old liberal domestic program has left liberalism as a forward thrust with nowhere to go, certainly no large design for the future. The old liberal feelings—protest and
indignation—seem to lack an adequate object. We no
longer talk about the "Liberal Imagination" but about
the "End of Ideology."

Among literary men, the old liberal attitudes have
survived chiefly in vigorous if isolated dissenters. Still,
our response to such dissent suggests the erosion and
retreat of the liberal tradition. Paul Goodman, who says

that choosing the lesser of two evils is false practicality, and Leslie Fiedler, who talks of the artist's duty to say no, are more likely to be regarded as cranks than as prophets. And no one is stirred when Kenneth Rexroth tells us, "It is impossible for an artist to remain true to himself as a man, let alone an artist, and work within the context of this society." [1]

The significant development of the nineteen-fifties has been repeatedly diagnosed as a movement away from alienation and towards reconciliation and accommodation. In America its prophets have been Lionel Trilling and David Riesman, the spokesman for autonomy. At this point we are no longer obsessed by the old antagonisms between self and society, or by the belief that hostility to society is the condition of integrity.

All this has left something of a cultural vacuum. The impressive flexibility of post-liberal intellectuals does not organize a party. The closest thing to an ideology now available is the new conservatism, at the moment hardly an impressive intellectual growth. Outside politics there have been existentialism and the new theological orthodoxy. Each has had a shaping effect on the imagination of a certain number of writers—Golding and John Barth, Walker Percy and Flannery O'Connor. A majority of thoughtful people, however, find themselves in a secular version of the Victorian predicament —they have lost their liberal faith and have not found any adequate substitute.

This condition has had a major effect upon our fiction. We expect it to be very closely in touch with reality—"a perpetual quest for reality, the field of its

research being always the social world" [2]—yet much of it
is out of touch with both the material and the temper of
our time. The imagination of liberalism, which was in
the past one of rebellion, of assertion of the self against
the restraints of the existing social and political order,
operated in fiction to produce realistic novels of social
documentation and novels which assert individual sensibility in a corrupt world. Both types were fixed a long
time ago, and both are in trouble now. Probably nothing is wrong with the genres themselves. But the imagination behind such novels and the literary conventions
governing them have not greatly altered in the face of
vastly changed social and political conditions. As a result
the novels deriving their impetus from this tradition are
today likely to have a tired, secondhand quality about
them; they seem to be responding to a condition no
longer existing, or responding to our present condition
in a way no longer relevant.

The novel of social documentation can hardly succeed
in portraying a social order essentially iniquitous when
its audience has ceased to give automatic assent to the
belief that society is innately hostile to individual fulfilment or human betterment. The novel of individual
sensibility represents the other side of the same proposi-
tion. In Chekhov's time the exploration of sensibility
was likely to be connected with hostility to organized
society. Individual sensibility was the alternative to the
obstructive force of society, and failure became almost a
proof of sensibility. Gradually, however, the exploration
of sensibility has become dissociated from protest, and
with the development of new techniques, such as stream

of consciousness, has come to be dominant in its own right.

While these novels of sensibility seem to have divorced themselves from general political-cultural concerns, they are dependent upon the old antagonistic individual-society disjunction. And as that disjunction has eroded, so these novels have become soggy or tedious investigations of fine feelings.

By an odd paradox liberalism has been allied to the prophetic strain in fiction. Although the best prophets— Dostoevsky, Lawrence—can hardly be called liberal, they have in their intensity, their concern with moral absolutes, been temperamentally close to the moral pulse of liberalism; they are in a sense its evangelical branch. Yet as absolutes and intensity have become suspect, the transforming visions of writers like Lawrence and Dostoevsky are more likely to be regarded as art rather than gospel.

There have been alternatives to these prolongations of earlier moods. Talented writers like James Thurber and Mary McCarthy, who in an earlier time might have put all their energies into the novel, have turned to exposition, travelogue, personal anecdote. Although this provides a pleasant relief from the ritualistically serious novel, it appears to be a way of avoiding engagement.

A more significant and promising alternative is the comic novel. Though the golden age of comedy predicted by Kingsley Amis [3] is still in the offing, there have been in the past decade or so a large number of good comic novels, by Amis, Wain, DeVries, Honor Tracy, Newby, and their followers. With most, comedy is not a way of avoiding engagement, but of exploring the basic assumptions of the debate going on in our culture.

Given this decline of ideology and the gradual shift away from alienation and the celebration of failure and toward accommodation and reconciliation, Snow is for many readers the right novelist for the time. Not because he is a prophet, but because he refuses to be a prophet; he is much too cagey, much too sparing of generalization, much too pragmatic. He is not on a quest for reconciliation. Nonetheless he has achieved a certain measure of it along the way and, as it were, piecemeal. Whatever the validity of such an approach, its openness, the range of material and experience it calls for, bring us into contact with the world around us more clearly than could those novels written in the liberal tradition.

What Snow has is neither a new version of the liberal ideology nor of its competitors but something fundamentally non-ideological—a tolerant, knowledgeable, worldly pragmatism. The test of its validity is in how well it enables Snow to deal with his subject matter. At one time or another he has touched on most of the subjects that have engaged us in the past four decades: the reforming and liberating spirit of the twenties; the conflict in the thirties over Spain and Nazism; the bomb; the narrowing of loyalties in the Cold War; and, most of all, the problems of power and conscience in the managerial society. And generally his treatment rings true. We feel that he is talking our language about our problems, that in a large way he sees what the problems are and the possible attitudes that can be adopted toward them.

Snow's hero and narrator Lewis Eliot begins as a liberal, but his scepticism, his knowledgeability, gradually lead him toward a revised and tempered liberalism. He abandons very early any belief in individual perfectibility and finds he cannot accept the liberal hopefulness of his friend George Passant. Eventually, when he finds himself part of the established management of power, he must sometimes defend it against liberal complaints— partly on the grounds that politics is the art of the possible, partly on the grounds that changed conditions have made some of the old liberal pieties anachronistic.

The progress of the hero-narrator is one that in fiction has usually led to perdition (as in *Great Expectations* and *Room at the Top*). What is notable in Snow is not a reversal of this (he refuses to turn the cliché on its head), but that Lewis Eliot is never entirely comfortable as a liberal in the twenties and thirties, never entirely easy as a man of power in the forties and fifties. He is deeply concerned with ideas and politics (and with a distinct liberal commitment), but he is more interested in human values and character, and therefore in individual cases. Thus he is continually discovering the inadequacy of general formulas: he finds that reactionaries may be in many ways most honorable men, and that liberals can be pompous and self-deceived. (The opposite possibilities occur too, but the exceptions to our expectations are more striking.)

Snow's views in general are equally flexible and open.

If we ask what he thinks about human nature, we can only answer that he thinks about it continuously and absorbedly, but that he is not given to categorizing. Are managers bad? Sometimes yes, sometimes no, it all depends. Are scientists naïve politically? It depends. As a theory this is probably hard to equal for banality; but Snow does not hold it as a theory. It is simply a loose description of his temper. What counts in a man of such a temper is force and intelligence. And that of course is the essential Snow: a remarkably shrewd and intelligent examiner of character and motive, in particular of the psychological and moral terms of middle-class professional life in our times.

In large part Snow's revision of liberalism turns on a frequently repeated distinction between individual and social life. Individual life is tragic: but this is no reason for us to give up social hope. In his sense of individual life Snow is not so far removed from those who talk about alienation, but he still retains many of the old liberal social goals (though tempered as to means). The distinction he makes does not seem difficult. But because of the linkage in the past between social hope and an optimistic view of human nature, and the linkage at present between disenchanted views of man and conservative views of society, Snow's position has not always been understood.

"Well, I suppose," says a somewhat reluctant critic, "he's important because he writes about those things which really matter." [4] Or, as Lionel Trilling put it, Snow's subject is "man in committee"—perhaps not a bad definition of one of the major matters available

to the novelist today. In part Snow's fiction exemplifies
the sociological truism that our sense of identity comes
most strongly from our jobs. Lewis Eliot's work is at the
center of his personal life, and is the source and occasion
of many of the moral crises which form his character. It
is through work that he meets his friends, and even his
relations with his brother are strongly affected by their
jobs. For him the people who have money and social
position are fortunate because such assets give them an
edge professionally. As we see Lewis Eliot at the various stages of his career, we always know exactly where
he stands in the professional hierarchy, where he is on
the ladder of success. This is true of even the minor
characters—they are identified in terms of their positions in professional and institutional hierarchies.
"Jones was over fifty, had just become a Deputy Secretary, and would not go further." [5] The wives are also
regularly described in terms of the degree to which they
help or hurt their husbands' positions. (This is not to
say that Snow thinks in terms of the values of a careerist
or personnel manager, but that his social observation
recognizes the importance of these things for his characters.)

In the past, the novel's concern with personal relations was generally worked out in terms of marriage.
Not that novelists were obsessed with marriage, but that
it was important for the characters and therefore for the
novelist. Even by the mid-nineteenth century jobs were
not particularly important in the novel, partly because
the characters couldn't be said to have jobs in our sense
of the word, partly because the novelist wanted to con-

centrate on a more limited range of personal relations. Lydgate's medical career in *Middlemarch,* Trollope's civil servants and his Prime Minister are the infrequent exceptions. To a considerable extent this has remained true in twentieth-century fiction. In *Howards End* the Wilcoxes stand for the "world of telegrams and anger," but mostly they stand for it. That world affects their personal relations, but we do not see the Wilcoxes running their business. Even Galsworthy (often called one of Snow's predecessors), though he tells us a good deal about how the love of property affects personal relations, gives us in *The Man of Property* only one scene in which the Forsytes conduct business; for the rest we get the traditional parties and gossip. Typically the hero in novels has been like Nick Carraway of *The Great Gatsby;* we are told that Nick is a bond salesman and that is all; in the novel we see him outside working hours involved with his neighbor, a cousin, a girl he meets at a party. Snow, for all his interest in careers, has not divorced himself from the tradition of the personal novel. Rather he has brought that tradition up to date, accommodated it to a world in which jobs have assumed an unprecedented importance.

Snow's preoccupation with careers has the effect of revivifying the personal novel. It also is a way of connecting personal concerns with something larger. And this aspect of Snow's work suggests what is happening to the political novel. The political novel has always had as its basic situation the point at which individual fates join with the larger movements of society, and its history reflects the changing definition of politics and the changing sense of the interrelation of the individual and society.

When Scott wrote *Old Mortality,* the matter was battles and external political events, and the issues for the characters were something like loyalty and integrity. Fifty years later, George Eliot in *Felix Holt* was not so much concerned with public events as with a sociological analysis of the constitution of society and of the formation of opinion. And most political novelists since Eliot have had this strong sociological bias. The transition from Scott to Eliot reflects the shift from the last era of the old internal wars of Europe to the age of industrialization and parliamentary democracy. Like the science of politics itself, the political novel followed this shift from the study of dramatic public events like treaties and wars to the study of the sociology of political action.

In Snow's novels we get a response to a new set of political conditions. In the past the sociological analysis was connected with Whig and Jeffersonian views of the diffusion of power. The political mythology which tells us to look to society as a whole to understand political action is still with us, but the pressure of events has brought about a change in the location of power and eventually an awareness of the importance of the behavior of a small group of politicians and administrators. And not surprisingly Snow turns his attention here too, for he can make a good case that these people are making the decisions for our society, and that this is a profitable area for the investigation of motive and conduct. It provides great possibilities for the analysis of character and at the same time is large and important to society as a whole.

Snow is, of course, not unique in having a sense for relevant material in our time, but he is unusual in having a relevant set of attitudes towards it. As it happens, these attitudes are much like those of an older tradition. In his concern for character as it manifests itself in social situation, and for social fact as the condition of character, Snow is very close to the English realistic tradition, the tradition of Jane Austen, George Eliot, Trollope, which sees that most of our significant ethical choices are worked out in the mundane and the trivial. Accompanying this horizontal way of examining moral reality is a worldly temperament—a fascination with the details of the everyday world, a tolerant, equable, pragmatic spirit, and, at its very best (with Jane Austen certainly), a combination of a sense of ethical complexity with an almost impassioned drive towards harmony. This spirit works not through ideas but through continuous scrutiny; it combines a maximum of openness with a drive towards resolution. At best it has an intense engagement with moral reality; at its worst it is flabby, a moral neutralism by default. And one of the major questions to be asked about Snow's novels is whether they have tension or simply slackness, whether his is the art of balance or of trimming.

At the moment I should like to put aside the qualitative question and simply identify some of the important attitudes in Snow's fiction. One of the most striking is Snow's attitude towards power and the desire for power. Oddly there is very little general discussion of power in the novels. One of the few general statements—in *The Light and the Dark*—is that power is too dangerous a thing to be in the hands of a few men (this in the context of an argument about the social efficiency of Nazism). Yet power is one of the largest presences in Snow's fiction, and it is presented simply as a fact. It is there, men struggle over it, it would be unreasonable to think of a world in which it was not important. It is to be looked at as clearly as possible, without preconceptions, without moral animus—certainly not in terms of clichés and abstractions about the Organization Man and the Establishment.

So also with ambition. Snow takes it to be a very large fact in the world he presents. It exists and it is worth looking at to see how it affects individuals, how it shapes their characters:

> He was so clever that he did not need to strain, but he intended to have Rose's success and more than Rose's success. My private guess was that he was for once over-estimating himself: nothing could prevent him doing well, one could bet on his honours, one could bet that he would go as high as Jones—but perhaps not higher. It might be that, in the next ten years when he was competing with the ablest, he would just lack the weight, the sheer animal force, to win the highest jobs.[6]

Snow's presentation of social fact has generally this quality, and his detachment is no doubt one of the things that has antagonized some of his readers, who feel that he ought to show more disapproval.

Snow is similarly matter-of-fact about human nature

and free both of censoriousness and of romantic surprise at evil. He simply starts out assuming that it is true that we are full of contradictions, that our motives are rarely perfect. As Lewis Eliot says of Arthur Brown, "Brown loved his friends, and knew they were only men." [7]

Snow is one of the most tolerant novelists in generations. With equal detachment he has presented and made humanly credible an industrial manager, a cabinet minister, a high-ranking civil servant, a scientist who gives secrets to spies, another scientist who breaks down the defecting scientist, people on both sides of the political divide of the thirties, and so on. Snow's openness and generosity of temperament are very closely connected with the fact that he is a great deal more interested in studying and understanding character than in judging it.

The set of attitudes that emerges in Snow's fiction is loose, amorphous, and pragmatic, and resists quick formulation. It emerges through a set of dialectical qualifications. His hero-narrator Lewis Eliot is one of those in the corridors of power, but he is a man remarkable for decency of feeling, imagination, and awareness of the limitations of the bureaucratic mind. And all that he experiences and reports is presented in terms of this tension. This sounds as if Lewis Eliot is making the best of both worlds, but in fact it is like the pragmatism of a mature judicial system, which carries on the business of justice not through enunciating universal dicta but by being open to all conflicting claims, and saying yes here, and no there, hoping gradually to find a course.

Thus we have Lewis Eliot the bureaucrat in one instance denouncing a committee's fondness for mediocrity in the selection of personnel, and shortly afterwards defending to an angry liberal the Government's policy in the atomic spy trials. A more complex and extensive case of this pragmatic dialectic appears in *The New Men*. During the course of the novel, the scientists become very concerned about the use of the atomic bomb: shall they take action? shall they break their oaths of secrecy to make a really effective protest? Lewis Eliot appears in the discussion as representative of the official cast of mind, agreeing with the scientists that something should be done but maintaining that breaking their oaths would not only be dishonorable but ineffective. After the War Lewis Eliot's younger brother, the hero of the novel, who has worked energetically in the bomb project, suddenly renounces his connection with the atomic establishment. Lewis Eliot comments:

> For any of us who had been concerned with the bomb . . . there was no clear-cut way out. . . . There were just two conceivable ways. One was the way he [the younger brother] had just taken: the other, to struggle on . . . and take our share of what had been done and what might still be done, and hope that we might come out at the end of the tunnel. Being well meaning all the time, and thinking of nothing worse than our own safety.
>
> He [the younger brother] meant that you could not compromise. If you accepted the bomb, the burnings alive, the secrets, the fighting point of power, you must take the consequences. . . . You were living in a power equilibrium, and you must not pretend; the relics of liberal humanism had no place there.[8]

Thus Lewis Eliot has made his choice, but made it reluctantly and only under the compulsion of events. His response can be described as muddling through—if you ignore the imagination, the fineness of personal and social conscience out of which it arises. While it is not very exciting as an abstract social policy, it has obviously a good deal of relevance to the individual who must make some decision on an issue. Indeed on a question like atomic weapons it is for many people the only course that allows them to preserve personal integrity and at the same time to meet the demands of political action.

With *Corridors of Power* some other possibilities begin to enter the series more explicitly. Up to this time the world of power has been treated sympathetically, more sympathetically than we are accustomed to in fiction. To some of his critics Snow seems all too much at ease in the corridors of power: he may be intelligent about how it works, how men get it; but he has too few reservations about power, too few questions. With *Corridors of Power* it appears that Snow has been biding his time in elaborating the full treatment of power that the structure of the series wants and that Snow hinted at in his prefatory statement to *The Conscience of the Rich*— "the love of power and the renunciation of power." Earlier in the series—in the history of Martin Eliot—we have caught glimpses, whose full import is not clear at the time, of the rejection of power.

Now, as part of the dialectic of the series, two things appear—a new kind of hero and some new attitudes toward power. Roger Quaife is neither a failure nor one of those men of the world who live by the definition of politics as the art of the possible. He has the toughness

and strength of the men of power but also an unmana-
gerial idealism, a desire to do good. Snow's men of
power compel admiration for their strength and their
freedom from the more dangerous illusions that frus-
trate action and destroy men. But they are finally and
crucially vulnerable to the charge of not wanting
enough, of identifying the possible with the world as it
is. Hence the importance of Roger, who is not satisfied
with the manipulation of the possible, who wants to
change the conditions of the possible. What the series
seems to be working towards is a sense that Lewis Eliot's
ethical stance (so far as we have seen it) is a reasonable,
an honorable way to be—but not necessarily the only
way to be. Prudence and worldliness are not discredited,
but we are beginning to see their costs and limitations—
and to be aware of an alternative in the world of power.

Along with this there is in *Corridors of Power* a shift
in the perspective in which power is seen. In the earlier
novels we have watched characters play the game of
power, seen the conflict of wills, the psychological tricks.
The game of power has been an important test of the
characters' integrity; and Snow has implied that since
power has social consequences this game is important.
We have not had many questions asked about the game
itself. Now Lewis Eliot begins to present it as just that, a
game, something that may be trivial, one fact in a larger
world. (There is a curious irony here since in *Corridors
of Power* the literal and historical stakes are great.)
Again and again in *Corridors of Power* Lewis Eliot
notes the characters' overvaluation of politics. He has
said all along that politics is the same in a college or a
cabinet; now, reflecting on a cabinet struggle, he com-

pares it to "a struggle on a pettier scale when I had been voting for a Master of my college."

In terms of questions about the meaning of human existence there is in Snow no equivalent to these considerations, for he does not raise questions of ultimate meaning, of why one lives. The one tragedy in the "Strangers and Brothers" series, *The Light and the Dark,* presents a hero who sees so clearly into the darkness of the human condition that he is driven to suicide. All the grounds of existential tragedy are acknowledged, but there is no formulation of the problem as such. The hero's perception of the desperateness of our condition is shown to be valuable, but on the practical level a grievous misfortune. Most of the time, however, such questions are clearly outside the bounds of the examination of human life in Snow's novels.

Snow's pragmatism and good sense are impressive when he deals with how one should live in the world; clearly they are not the equipment for dealing with ultimate questions. Snow's decision as to what kind of novel he should write is thus a wise one. While there is a sense in which readers may compare him with writers like Camus, Golding, Styron, there is no particular reason why he should write their kind of novel, and the only way in which such different kinds of writers can be compared is in terms of the insight and art that each brings to his peculiar subject. Snow knows where his strength is, in his fascinated and intelligent account of how the world works and how one can and should live in it. His is a moral imagination, not a theological or existential one.

3 ❧

The "Strangers and Brothers" Sequence

THE fact that Snow is writing a series regularly attracts comment and produces references to other series, to Balzac, Proust, Galsworthy. But there has not been much critical examination of Snow's series as such. The fact that it is incomplete justifies a wait-and-see policy. But I suspect too that we do not quite know what to make of a series, that it goes against our feeling about the autonomy of the individual work of art.

In the next chapter I shall say something about the architectonic of the series as a whole. For the moment we can follow the lead of publishers who assure us on the dust jackets that each novel is complete and independent.

Since several of the novels are set later than 1935, the time when Snow first thought of the series, one assumes that the plan was somewhat general. " 'I knew where I was going to begin and where I was going to end—human fatalities apart—and a good deal of the intervening territory I needed to cover. . . . I wasn't sure then of the number of volumes but the present scope was, in essence, present in my mind.' " [1] For some time Snow has described the series as comprising eleven volumes, of which at this point nine have been published. The first volume, *Strangers and Brothers,* was published in 1940. Since the War the novels have been appearing regularly at approximately two-year intervals:

Strangers and Brothers	1940
The Light and the Dark	1947
Time of Hope	1949
The Masters	1951
The New Men	1954
Homecoming	1956
The Conscience of the Rich	1958
The Affair	1960
Corridors of Power	1964

What remains is *The Devoted* and another novel, as yet untitled, which will "round off the series."

Snow has classified his novels into those of "direct experience" and of "observed experience," that is, the two (eventually three) in which Lewis Eliot is the hero, and the other novels in which he is chiefly observer and narrator.[2]

The novels of observed experience might usefully be divided, though the division is not too sharp, into those

which focus on a central hero and those which focus
on a group or society. *The Light and the Dark* and
The Conscience of the Rich center on individual heroes. *The Masters* and *The Affair,* on the other hand,
are without a hero unless we say the group is hero.
Strangers and Brothers, The New Men and *Corridors of
Power* divide their focus between an individual hero
and the study of a group.

Though Snow does not claim to present a portrait of
an age, the scope of the novels gives us something like a
picture of the professional and intellectual classes in
England from the twenties through the fifties. In part,
Snow's portrait gives the timeless conditions of professional life—the young man on the way up, the conflict of
wills in committee, the office clerk calculating the prospects of the barristers. But much of his portrait reflects
the social and political climate of the times—the ferment
of the twenties, the political divide of the thirties, the
War, and then the Cold War and its social, political and
intellectual by-products. And Snow's practical intelligence and reluctance to blame make this portrait remarkable.

More particularly, the "Strangers and Brothers" series
gives us a sense of the moral and psychological temper of
the "new men," the inhabitants of a world increasingly
professionalized and bureaucratized, a world in which
talent and ambition have become more important than
property and the traditional advantages.

In the realm of personal relations the world of "Strangers and Brothers" is one in which the traditional relationships of family and family connections and of class

seem relatively unimportant (Lewis Eliot's family ceases to be important to him once he is grown up, and his brother is no more than mentioned until he has been established as a professional man). In the place of the traditional relationships there is a great intensification of self-achieved relationships—of friendship, love—and Snow scrutinizes them in great detail. This is part of what is implied in the general title of "Strangers and Brothers," and it would appear that it is the strangers who can most readily become brothers.

Strangers and Brothers (1940), the first novel of the series, marks one of those steps in the development of an author in which he seems to go back a bit in the process of going forward. It is, I think, the least impressive of the sequence, and its troubles suggest that after *The Search* Snow's art was undergoing some fundamental changes. *Strangers and Brothers* presents a group of young people in a provincial town. Their stirrings of new life and personal ambition are encouraged and stimulated by the hero George Passant, a warm and impatient man. He makes brothers out of several, including the narrator, who would otherwise be strangers.

What the title of the novel points to is our aloneness, and the way in which a man like George can make a brother of a stranger. George Passant, a solicitor's clerk with much greater talents than prospects, wants little for himself but does want to help his friends. He becomes involved in an investment scheme in the course of which erroneous or falsified figures are used to attract investors. In the last part of the novel the hero and his friends are tried for fraud. Lewis Eliot, who has left the town and become a barrister, returns to defend them. Gradually he discovers that the idealistic solicitor has knowingly engaged in fraud. More generally, the novel explores the hero's self-deception and the taint of possessiveness in his generosity to his friends.

In *The Search* Snow had handled his narrative fairly well. But in *Strangers and Brothers,* in which he was developing his peculiar approach to the study of character, he was unable to keep in balance the movement of plot and the inward change in the characters. As a result the novel moves very slowly; in the latter part the action stands still while we explore the character of George Passant.

For all of the effort expended on characterization, all but a few of the people in *Strangers and Brothers* are somewhat nebulous. George is much more successfully realized in *Homecoming,* where he is much less important; and his relations with Lewis Eliot are much sharper and clearer in *Time of Hope* than in *Strangers and Brothers.* In *Strangers and Brothers* George's warmth and diffidence are more asserted than demonstrated. The extensive use of George's diary is a weak expedient that suggests Snow's perplexity as to how to present him. Jack Cotery, Olive, Morcom, all seem indefinite; between a few surface mannerisms and a great deal of analysis there is nothing in the middle. The analytical swamps the dramatic; that is to say, Snow does not, as he will do later, build his novel by means of chapter-length dramatic scenes which are capable of accommodating and pointing up the analysis.

Still, there is much of the familiar Snow material in

Strangers and Brothers: the committee-meeting, the fretting at motive, the understated chapter titles ("A Cup of Coffee Spilt in a Drawing-Room"), and many passages of analysis that might have come from almost any of Snow's novels:

> "I believe that," said Calvert. A glance of sympathy passed between them; for a second, they were made intimate by their quarrel. Then Calvert said obstinately: "But it has nothing to do with it." [3]

> She was speaking from a double motive, of course; her dislike for the Principal shone out of her: so did her desire to help George. [4]

There is the quick outline of the state of things in the committee:

> It was still one against four, if it came to a vote; but there was a curious, hypercharged atmosphere that even the absolute recalcitrants . . . felt as they became more angry. Over Beddow and Martineau certainly, the two most receptive people there, had come a jag of apprehension. [5]

And we find already a formula which Snow uses repeatedly in character description:

> For all her passions of subjection, she actually—in another aspect of her nature—was a strong and masterful person. [6]

The second novel of the series, *The Light and the Dark* (1947), constitutes a pair with *Strangers and Brothers.* The hero, Roy Calvert, like George Passant, becomes a brother for Lewis Eliot. But in every other

respect he is the opposite of George. Roy Calvert is
wealthy and brilliant and has much personal charm.
Where George Passant, for all his hopefulness, is ultimately without prospects in the world, Roy Calvert
achieves a considerable reputation as a scholar at Cambridge. Where George Passant is self-deceived and optimistic, Roy Calvert is without illusion and without
hope. His clarity of vision makes him unable to commit
himself. The novel records his alternating moods of despair and high spirits, and his quest—for religious belief,
for political faith, for something in which to lose himself.

The emphasis is not on the quest, for there is really
no possibility that Roy can escape from his despair. The
novel thus faces the same technical problem, the analysis
of a static character, that troubled *Strangers and Brothers*. But by this time Snow is able to manage the problem (between the publication of *Strangers and Brothers*
and *The Light and the Dark* he had written but not
published *The Masters*).[7] With a good deal of ingen-
ious contrivance he keeps us and Lewis Eliot wondering
what the hero will do next. Whether he will remain in
one of his calm moods or lapse into despair again?
Whether his desperation will drive him to some freak or
prank? Whether his conduct will hurt the fellows' cam-
paign for the election of a new Master? By this means
Snow has enlarged the scope of the novel beyond the
immediate concern with the hero, and has employed a
good deal of external suspense to keep things in motion.

For the first time we get something that will become a
standard feature in Snow's novels, the cast of memorable

minor characters, in this case the women who love Roy Calvert, his aristocratic friends, and the remarkably varied group of fellows in the college. The minor characters, in contrast to those of *Strangers and Brothers,* are sharply individualized. Generally too there is a great deal more local dramatic conflict—meetings, dinners, and parties that have life and interest in themselves and are not simply occasions for the analysis of character. *The Light and the Dark* contains more description than any of the other novels, and much atmosphere which supports the hero's moods of despair.

One guesses that after the troubles of *Strangers and Brothers,* Snow turned first to the writing of *The Masters* (which was composed second but published fourth in the series), a novel which has no hero but a great deal of social notation. He then returned to a more conventional kind of novel in *The Light and the Dark,* seeking to find in it room for the examination of the individual hero and for the observation of society. The fusion is not perfect in *The Light and the Dark,* but with it Snow found the general formula for most of the novels that followed. In the process he seems to have become more sure of the nature of his gifts as a novelist.

The title of *The Light and the Dark* is as close as Snow ever comes to the symbolic. Specifically it refers to the hero's researches into Manichean texts and more generally to his moods of gaiety and despair. In the largest way it suggests the darkness of the human situation and the possible alternatives for dealing with it— religious faith, political ideology.

In its hero and theme *The Light and the Dark* is the

least typical of Snow's novels, and the most like the an-
guished explorations of values that have been so common in twentieth-century fiction. For although the
novel does not endorse the hero's despair, it makes us,
through its patient and sympathetic narrator, take Roy
Calvert's experience seriously. If Roy Calvert is something of a Meursault, Snow is no Camus. The hero com-
mands our imaginative sympathy. But it is Lewis Eliot
who tells the story, and one has the feeling that since he
sympathizes with his friend but does not despair himself, then perhaps Roy Calvert's experience is the result
of a flaw in him rather than in the nature of reality.

The hero's melancholy is somewhere between the
romantic and the existential:

> This special melancholy, this clear-sighted despair in
> which, more than anyone I knew, he saw the sadness
> of man's condition: this despair which drove him to
> outbursts of maniacal gaiety. He was born with this
> melancholy; it was a curse of fate, like an hereditary
> disease. It shadowed all his life. Perhaps it also deep-
> ened him under his caprices, perhaps it helped to
> make him the most selfless of men.[8]

The quotation suggests one of the minor troubles of the
novel, an extravagant rhetoric: "inexplicable misery";
"none of them saw the weight that crushed him down";
"the special melancholy which belongs to some chosen
natures." [9] For all that, Roy Calvert is a largely successful creation, and we are not indifferent before his fate.

Snow seems more interested in observing, understanding, sympathizing, than in tracing things down to
origins (hence the deliberate vagueness of "like an he-

reditary disease") or in pressing for ultimates. The reader who is conditioned to writers like Kafka, Golding, and Bowles may be surprised at Snow's deliberately stopping short. Not long before the hero's death (he becomes an R.A.F. bomber pilot knowing that he will die), we are told that his melancholy has become worse, his choice irrevocable. "It gave no time for the obstinate hope of the fibres, which underlay even his dark vision of the mortal state, to collect itself, steady him, and help him to struggle on." [10] In contrast to Roy Calvert, Lewis Eliot has the "hope of the fibres," or as Roy Calvert calls it "idiot hope." [11] Neither here nor elsewhere does Snow really develop the questions raised by this kind of contrast or look for the significance of such experiences as Roy Calvert's. Hope is obviously a desirable thing, Roy Calvert's suffering is terrible and deserves our compassion. Snow chooses not to explore the larger and deeper questions of why men live and why they should. And to write Snow's kind of novel, which is fascinated with how men live, it is probably necessary to ignore such questions. Most readers will not quarrel with his choice of subject matter. But what is troublesome is that a number of things in *The Light and the Dark* seem to make such questions almost unavoidable.

Time of Hope, the third novel in the series (1949), involves another kind of change. It is the first novel in which Lewis Eliot himself is the hero. It is a much tighter novel than its two predecessors, with all of its events integrated into the story of the narrator-hero. Since *Time of Hope* is best discussed in connection with its sequel *Homecoming* (1956), I would like to move to the fourth novel of the "Strangers and Brothers" sequence, *The Masters,* which was written second but was not published until 1951.

The Masters did a great deal to make Snow's reputation, particularly in America. It was awarded the James Tait Black Memorial Prize (together with *The New Men*) and has been universally admired. On several counts *The Masters* is a remarkable novel. For many critics it is the best in the series, and it is probably the most intelligent academic novel ever written. It is also a fascinating and brilliant portrait gallery, a singular *tour de force,* and of course a preliminary study of the workings of power. Using to the utmost his sense of character, his knowledgeability, and his talent for creating suspense, Snow has constructed an immensely absorbing novel which has no hero and no explicit theme, and the reader hardly notices the absence of either.

The Masters, like *The Light and the Dark,* has a Cambridge setting and covers some of the same time and incidents. What Trollope thought was good for only a chapter ("Who Will Be the Next Bishop?") is the mainspring of *The Masters.* At the opening of the novel the current Master is dying of cancer and the thirteen members of the college begin to plan the election of a successor. At the end of the novel a Master has finally been elected. Even people contemptuous of what-happens-next as a principle in novel writing have testified to the absorbed curiosity with which they read *The Masters.* If we exclude detective and suspense story writing, probably the only other living author of whom this might be said is Graham Greene.

What is a partial solution and palliative in *The Light and the Dark* is the substance of *The Masters:* the suspenseful plot, the fascinated analysis of a small group, the presentation of a gallery of characters. It is not difficult to recall each of the members of the college distinctly and with pleasure: the narrator; his friend Roy Calvert; Brown the natural manager; Brown's ally Chrystal, who likes to manage too but is more eager for action; Luke, the youngest fellow, a scientist who has no doubts about supporting the non-scientist as candidate; in the opposing party, Despard-Smith, the aged censorious clergyman; Winslow, bitter and disappointed; Nightingale, the failure as a scientist, bitter but lacking the integrity and honor of Winslow; Pilbrow the liberal man of letters; Gay, the vain and eccentric authority on the Icelandic sagas; Francis Getliffe, the intense and high-minded liberal scientist. And the two candidates for Master: Jago, warm, imaginative, thin-skinned; and Crawford, the distinguished scientist and political liberal, sober, somewhat pompous.

Essentially the novel consists of a series of caucuses in the fellows' rooms, exchanges in the combination room, attempts to win over a vote, and speculations on the odds. In this respect, *The Masters* is similar to *Strangers and Brothers*. But in *The Masters* the characters are clearly individualized, and each meeting provides its own conflict and contributes still more urgency to the question of who will be elected. With a very sure hand Snow maintains suspense, so that we do not get all the votes accounted for until late in the novel, and the switch that frustrates the narrator and the reader is sprung on us only near the end.

The large political context is the international politics of 1937, and one of the divisions that strongly affects the election is politics. Given these issues, which the novel takes very seriously, Snow is remarkable for his tolerance. In the fourteen years between the events and the publication of the novel it would have been tempting to allot praise and blame in the light of history. And in any case, the spectacle of so many petty ambitions and small jealousies, so much ill-concealed desire for power and for revenge—this could be presented as contemptible irresponsibility. But Snow loves his characters too much for this, and he loves them too much as individuals to denounce them for their mistaken political or personal allegiances.

Although the War is in the offing and although the Mastership is important, Snow is neither shocked nor surprised at the machinations of college politics. Rather he is fascinated. Sooner or later a discussion of Snow must quote a passage which is nearly canonical now in criticism of his fiction. Near the end of *The Masters*, Brown's friend and co-manager Chrystal suddenly and impulsively changes his vote. Jago, who will now lose the election, says of him:

> "But he's more detestable than any of the others."
> "It's natural for you to say so," said Brown. "But it isn't true."
> "Are you going to trust him again?"
> Brown gave a sad, ironic, firm-hearted smile: I

thought it meant that he would trust Chrystal as much or as little as he had trusted him before. For Brown loved his friends, and knew they were only men. Since they were only men, they could be treacherous—and then next time loyal beyond belief. One took them as they were. That gave Brown his unfailing strength, and also a tinge, deep under the comfortable flesh, of ironic sadness.[12]

If "ironic sadness" is altered to something like "fascinated preoccupation with human variety," the passage comes close to describing Snow's own attitude, and what I suspect is the central secret of his success as a novelist.

It is not surprising that *The Masters* was reviewed in the *Public Administration Review*.[13] Indeed anyone interested in understanding how groups of managers and professional men operate, how decisions are made, could profitably study *The Masters,* for it presents a microcosm of all larger power structures. That is not why one reads *The Masters,* but there is much to be said for understanding how organizations work, to say nothing of acquiring greater understanding of human frailty in such situations.

The Affair (1960) ought to be looked at with *The Masters,* for it is in many ways the same kind of novel, with a slightly altered situation, a later time setting, and some new members in the cast of characters. Structurally it is quite similar to *The Masters:* it is a novel about a group rather than about an individual hero, and its plot depends on the group's decision. In place of "Who will be the next Master?", the question is "Will the college reverse its dismissal of a former fellow?" Its

situation is even more carefully balanced than that of
The Masters. The former fellow is both uninteresting
and unpleasant, and he is a militant Communist sympa-
thizer. His offense has been the grave one of fraud in the
publication of scientific research. Although he insists on
his innocence, he can offer no satisfactory explanation
for the falsification in the research results. The narrator,
Lewis Eliot (who is no longer a fellow but retains connections with his old college), becomes persuaded that
the college ought to reopen the case. As some complex
and puzzling new evidence turns up, the college gradually finds itself forced to hold a re-hearing. But the evidence is by no means clear-cut either way, and so we are
in suspense until the end, when the fellow is given min-
imum redress.

As in *The Masters*, the numerous turns and complica-
tions afford an opportunity for the familiar meetings
and caucuses and for the shrewd and tolerant examination of the tangle and complexity of individual motives.

Many of the characters from *The Masters* appear
again in *The Affair:* Brown the cautious and capable
academic manager; Winslow the sharp-tongued member
of the opposition; Crawford the eminent man of science,
who has turned out to be tolerably successful as Master;
Getliffe, now Sir Francis, still a man of high principle
and delicate conscience; and Lewis Eliot's brother
Martin, who is now a fellow.

As in *The Masters*, the immediate practical question
is set in a large political context, in this case (the time
setting of the novel is 1953–54) not the issues of Euro-
pean politics but the resurgence of the political right

and religious orthodoxy and the growth of political in-
differentism. The conservatives in *The Masters* were
simply anachronistic; those in *The Affair* represent a
new and militant force (and account for the majority of
the younger fellows at the college). The old secular liberals, Lewis Eliot and his brother, no longer represent
the forces of an embattled minority. Though Snow does
not press the point, they and their point of view are now
established and middle-aged.

Snow has done well with the twenties and brilliantly
with the thirties and forties. But in *The Affair* his imagination fails him somewhat when he attempts to present the mood of the fifties (something he does well in
Corridors of Power). His conservatives and his indiffer-
entists in *The Affair* are presented on the whole as a
fairly unlovely crew (which surely is a plausible view).
But Snow does not seem to have made the energetic
effort of imagination which made the characters of the
political reactionaries of the earlier novels triumphs of
insight and tolerance. The a-political Ince, for example,
seems to have been seen almost wholly in political terms
—in which there is nothing to be said for him—rather
than in the multiple perspectives of the earlier novels in
which political irresponsibility or wrongheadedness was
one of many human qualities. Snow in *The Light and
the Dark* scarcely agreed with Lord Boscastle's prepos-
terous social and political views. But he had seen him
also as an interesting character; Ince he sees only as a
danger.

In a sense *The Affair* is an investigation into justice.
But in no sense does it ask or answer the question

"What is justice?" It assumes that we know what justice is and proceeds to a question that is in one sense more important, "How do men go about the business of attaining justice?" There is of course no answer to this except by means of a combination of all that we are and know, our abstractions and our prejudices, the inevitable frictions and counter-responses of social life.

The Affair is thus a novel which must concern itself with character and with social processes, and as such it assumes a fixed set of moral standards. In this respect Snow belongs with an older literary tradition, not with the more recent one which rejects "fixed morality" for the attempt to discover moral value, which emphasizes abstraction rather than character. Snow is obviously more interested in character than in moral generalization. But he is not interested simply in individual moral choice. Between individual character on the one hand and justice as a legal metaphysical notion on the other, Snow sees and is interested in a third term, social process.

In *The Affair,* Snow looks at a particularly complex problem in a variety of dimensions: in terms of evidence; and since the evidence is not absolutely decisive, in terms of religious, political, and social attitudes; and also in terms of the temperaments and motives of the members of the college. (Lewis Eliot reflects on the resemblance of "the affair" to the Dreyfus case.) Snow explores a large number of combinations and permutations of these elements. One of the initial proponents of a reversal of the dismissal is a conservative; one of the early opponents is the liberal scientist Getliffe. Brown and Martin Eliot, the two opposed managers, are both cautious political men. The two fellows who believe *a priori* that a Communist cannot be trusted end up on opposite sides. At the end of *The Affair* we do not know any more about the nature of justice, but we are much more aware of the ways in which society goes about achieving justice.

The quality of the writing in *The Affair* is in many ways more assured than that of *The Masters*. But as a whole it is not quite so good a book as *The Masters*, perhaps because Snow is to some extent repeating himself. Some of the new people are quite good, and the familiar ones perform in character, though with less surprise and delight on the part of the reader. But taken as a whole, the group does not make the same indelible impress on the mind or strike us so much with the spectacle of human variety, nor is the suspense equal to that of *The Masters*.

The New Men, the fifth novel in the sequence, was published in 1954, three years after *The Masters*. It covers the years 1939 to 1946, from the first rumors of the atomic bomb to the successful operation of a pile, and it concerns itself with the groups of scientists and bureaucrats involved in this work. The main character is Lewis Eliot's younger brother Martin, one of the scientists. *The New Men*, like *The Masters*, studies the interaction of a group. It presents the planning and arguments about the bomb (Who will get the contract? Which research team should be backed?), and the group's response to the moral crisis of the bomb.

It is also, like *The Light and the Dark* and *Strangers and Brothers*, a novel about an individual's moral history. Martin Eliot is not remarkable as a scientist but has considerable talent as a manager—"cautious, subtle and far-sighted." [14] Though there is suspense about the project itself, the central interest is in Martin's career among the scientific bosses. When the scientists want to protest against the use of the bomb, Martin realistically proposes that the scientists can do nothing effective at this point and that they should wait and not lose influence by rashness. Not long after, when the War is ended, he determines to engage in just that kind of rashness (a letter of protest against the use of the bomb), although it will destroy his career. Lewis Eliot persuades him not to send the letter, and Martin turns back to the struggle for power in the scientific establishment. He rises in the esteem of the bureaucracy as he commits himself to the detection and breaking down of a defecting scientist. His toughness and foresight have at this point made him a candidate for the top job in the atomic establishment. But in the end he turns down the job, and the rejection is terrible for him. At the end of the novel he is seen as a tragic figure, a man who cannot reconcile power and conscience:

> Martin had not gone back on his choice, although by this time he knew, what one can never imagine until one lives it, the wear and tear, hour by hour and day by day, as one tries to reshape a life. . . .
> He believed now that his critics were right: from every practical point of view, his choice had been

stupid: he would stay there, doing his college teaching, without a realistic chance of achievement for the rest of his life.

He had always been quiet, but in the days of his power it had been the quietness, trained and confident, of a high functionary, the quietness of Hector Rose. Now it had changed; it had the special quality that you see in one who has learned something from life and who has lost his high spirits during the lesson. His interest had become passive. Sitting in the darkness of his room, looking out of the window at the court brilliant in the rain-clear sunlight, he had none of the authority of action that men like Luke carried on their brow.[15]

The two dimensions of the novel, the study of the group and the study of Martin Eliot, are very closely related, much more so than in *The Light and the Dark,* where the group constitutes an independent center of interest, interwoven with the account of Roy Calvert's despair. Martin is interested in power as Roy Calvert had not been, so his history must be worked out in terms of the group of scientists with whom he is associated.

Martin Eliot is one of a number of different types of men of power in Snow's novels—Brown, the academic manager who is a "genuinely humble man"; Bevill, the cautious old minister who has never revealed a secret or said anything bright and cutting; Sir Hector Rose, the perfect administrator; Lufkin, the tycoon; and of course Lewis Eliot himself.

Martin Eliot's problems are partly those of personal conscience, problems that any ambitious man might face: but his problems involve a larger question for our times. The possible answers range from complete rejection of atomic weapons to unhesitating acceptance. One of the scientists feels, "Either you retired and helped to leave your country defenceless. Or you made a weapon which might burn men, women and children in tens of thousands. What was a man to do?" Another scientist says, " 'I don't think we've got any option . . . we've got to make the infernal thing.' " [16] And in reading the book we are driven to ask questions about our historical situation, questions which have no completely satisfactory answer.

Martin Eliot is one of those complex natures Snow is interested in. Martin can be tough, opportunistic; we do not like him very much; and yet we cannot call him bad. And we must respect the fact that he is capable of conflict, as opposed to those for whom there is no problem within themselves about atomic weapons. Martin and another scientist are discussing whether the bomb will be used.

"I think it is incredible," said Martin.

His voice was harsh. He was more moved than Mounteney who, despite his cantankerousness, was a gentle man, to whom any kind of cruelty seemed like a visitation from another planet. Mounteney had never had to struggle with a sadic strain in his own nature. It is men who have had to struggle so who hate cruelty most. Suddenly, listening to the revulsion in Martin's voice, I knew he was one of them.[17]

In the course of the novel Martin Eliot and his brother disagree over the importance of success and happiness and the extent to which one should go in seeking power. The conflict between the two brothers is important for the whole series. For *The New Men* works with one of its larger themes, possessive love. We discover that Lewis Eliot's concern for his brother is, for all its good will, tainted with possessiveness and that part of Martin's development lies in breaking away from his brother's concern. Thus *The New Men* is thematically closer than the other novels of "observed experience" to Lewis Eliot's own history, and it carries one of the large *motifs* of the series. In the first novel, *Strangers and Brothers,* we saw strangers who were made brothers; in *The New Men* we see brothers who become strangers before they can become brothers again on a new basis.

The Conscience of the Rich (1958), the seventh novel of the series, has affinities with *The Masters* and *The Affair* in its delicately balanced moral question, with *The New Men* and the novels about Lewis Eliot in the theme of possessive love, and with *The New Men* and *The Light and the Dark* in the character of its hero.

The Conscience of the Rich covers the years 1927–36. Its hero, Charles March, is the son of a wealthy Jewish family. Against their violent opposition, he gives up a promising career at the bar to become a family doctor. Like Roy Calvert in *The Light and the Dark* and Martin Eliot in *The New Men* Charles March is one of those who has to struggle with his own nature. He chooses renunciation:

He knew . . . what it was like to be cruel. To be impelled to be cruel, and to enjoy it. Other young men could let it ride, could take themselves for granted, but not he. He could not accept it as part of himself. It had to be watched and guarded against. With the force, freshness and hope of which he was capable, he longed to put it aside, to be kind and selfless. . . . When he spoke of wanting to lead a "useful" life, he really meant something stronger. . . . What he really meant was "good." . . .

I sometimes thought it was those who were tempted to be cruel who most wanted to be good.[18]

Charles March's renunciation comes partly from this desire for goodness, partly from a manifestation of the "sick conscience of the rich." But his conflict is also with his father's possessive love; Charles wants to love his father but also to be free, and the father loves his son but cannot let him be free. For Mr. March had very early withdrawn, and he desires for his son the success he never fought for himself. As in *The New Men, Time of Hope,* and *Homecoming,* selfish and selfless love are bound up and often indistinguishable.

Some reviewers praised *The Conscience of the Rich* as Snow's best novel. I do not think it is the equal of *Homecoming. The Conscience of the Rich* has traces of the problems of the first two novels: the analysis of the hero is static; and the novel tends to sag in the middle. What the reviewers were pointing to, I think, was a certain shift in the direction of Snow's art. *The Conscience of the Rich* is much richer in atmosphere than the other novels, and in Mr. March, the hero's father,

Snow gives us a delightful eccentric, characterized by extravagance of manner. Mr. March is full of prejudices and small obsessions and talks in a total recall style, which continuously branches into irrelevant detail. As a result *The Conscience of the Rich* is a more acceptable novel to those who complain about the flatness of Snow's style and about the obsessive concern with professional life in his other novels. It is a more conventional novel but a little less a Snow novel.

The plot of *Corridors of Power* (1964), like that of most of the other novels, arises out of the interaction of personal and public concerns. The personal concerns are ambition, boldness, and the desire to do good, in Roger Quaife, a member of Parliament who becomes a Minister during the course of the novel. The public concern is the debate over the possibility of a reduction in nuclear weapons in the second half of the fifties. The Roger Quaife of the beginning of the book is ambitious, known as a comer. In addition to his ambition, or perhaps as part of it, he becomes interested in reducing armaments. From this flows the action of the novel. Very carefully Roger feels his way—sounding out scientists, looking for allies, seeking to become a Minister himself, anticipating objections a year ahead, softening up potential enemies, watching his step so as not to make enemies or reveal too much of his intentions. The climax of all this is a parliamentary debate over a White Paper on weapons policy.

The plot of *Corridors of Power,* as Snow tells us in the prefatory "Note," turns on an "unresolvable complication." There is no simple answer to questions about the timing and the vigor with which proposals for the reduction of armaments could effectively have been pushed in the period 1955–58. The novel's internal complication, too, is unresolvable—Roger's combination of ambition and idealism, of prudence and boldness. He says to Lewis Eliot, " 'The first thing is to get power. The next—is to do something with it.' " Getting power includes for Roger campaigning against his superior, knowing when to keep his mouth shut (he does not protest about Suez). Roger's conduct is not always admirable, and his opponents call him an adventurer, but his actions are defensible in terms of the general principle.

In the latter part of the book, the movement is reversed. Roger, who wants not only to stay in the cabinet but ultimately to become Prime Minister, is faced with the choice between acting upon his conviction and holding on to power. He is warned that the country is not ready for his policy now, that presenting it will mean defeat, that waiting a few years will be more effective. Roger can graciously and conscientiously retreat from his desire to act. Retreat seems sensible, but he does not do so. He is driven by hope, conviction, passion, the need to be something more than a man of prudence. Again at the end of the novel after his policy has been rejected he has the chance of backing down, of waiting for a better time. But once more he refuses, and the man who aimed for and perhaps had a chance of becoming Prime Minister is politically ruined. It is not a very romantic picture of the world well lost for conscience, but Roger's risk-taking is as defensible and morally more admirable than his earlier prudence. (Lewis Eliot, who has been his ally all along, resigns in sympathy.)

The unresolvable complication gives us one of those nicely balanced situations which allow the novelist to explore the ways in which character and circumstance interact; which allow him to examine minutely and faithfully the variety of slightly differing responses to the same situation. The novel offers in the minor characters a series of variations of the themes of ambition, integrity, and power. The Old Hero with his simple and dangerous integrity. Leverett-Smith, Roger's Parliamentary Secretary, who has little enthusiasm but cannot imagine anything other than supporting him and resigning with him (in contrast, Roger in the same position earlier had worked for the downfall of his Minister). In another contrast, Roger's friend and ally, Monty Cave, resigns over Suez, but fails to support Roger on armament reduction, when he sees that Roger is going to lose.

Corridors of Power illustrates the way in which the "Strangers and Brothers" sequence is able to incorporate situations that could not have been part of its original scheme. But the thematic matter of the novel is obviously an essential part of the total design. We have seen earlier (in *Time of Hope* especially) the early phase of the cycle of ambition and the pursuit of power. Snow has evidently had in mind for a long time the completion of this cycle.

In formal terms *Corridors of Power* is nearest to *Conscience of the Rich* and *The New Men*—a novel with an individual hero whose history is set in a rich social and political context, with which it divides interest. Just as in *The New Men* Martin Eliot's tragedy is presented within the workings of the scientific establishment, so here Roger's ambition is presented within a parliamentary setting. And as *The New Men* illustrates the workings of closed politics, so *Corridors of Power* illustrates the interaction of open and closed politics. One can see the desire for comprehensiveness, but one wonders if Snow's greatest gift, his psychological acumen, is not best suited to the workings of closed politics, in which character and the interplay of character are almost everything.

In any case Roger seems to me one of the less impressive of Snow's heroes. We remain not only outside him but at such a distance that his character seems insufficiently defined. There is nothing dull or unimportant in Roger's ambition, his desire to do good, or his failure, but the novel does not make us feel these things enough. It is tragic only in a schematic way. Perhaps the difficulty is that much of the time the novel does not focus on Roger and his internal conflict. In terms of his character, there is a beginning and an end but not enough to sustain the middle.

Curiously some of the minor characters, always a great strength in Snow, suffer from something of the same difficulty. Cave, whose boldness reproaches Roger at the beginning, and whose prudence contrasts with Roger's courage at the end, is promising, but with him and with other minor characters we do not get on either the intuitive or the analytical level a strong sense of what makes them act the way they do. On the other hand, some of the characters whom we have seen in the earlier novels perform splendidly and even offer surprises for us.

Time of Hope (1949), the third book of the series, and *Homecoming* (1956), the sixth, should be considered together. In these two novels Lewis Eliot tells his own history (which will be completed in a third novel). Of all the novels in the series, these two have the strongest dramatic progression and the closest fusion between plot and character. They constitute a single story which is at the center of the whole "Strangers and Brothers" sequence.

Time of Hope is a young-man-from-the-provinces novel, accommodated to the conditions of the first third of the twentieth century. Its hero, Lewis Eliot, comes from a lower middle-class family with aspirations to gentility. Lewis Eliot is seen as he rises in the world, rejecting the relatively safe prospect of becoming a solicitor for a precarious chance for a career at the bar. Part of the "hope" of the title is his mother's fierce, possessive desire that her son should do well and rise in the world. Part of it is the narrator's own ambition. Here, more than in the other novels, the suspense is integral to the growth of the main character. We wonder whether Lewis Eliot will be able to afford to study for the bar. Whether he will be able to do well enough in the examination to get a start. Whether he will make enough money at the bar. Whether Sheila will marry him.

As in the other novels, Snow explores the problem of ambition—not only in Lewis Eliot, but in George Passant; in Mr. Knight, whose lack of achievement gives him a curious satisfaction and a detached fascination with the success of others; and in Herbert Getliffe, the shifty and mercurial barrister. And one of the notable things about this is that Snow is quite free from romanticizing ambition and equally free from the more common sentimental revulsion against it. Ambition is a fact in the world; it is part of a man's nature; the best one can do is to understand his nature and come to terms with it. To have such a nature may not be convenient; to come to terms with it may be costly.

Early in the novel Lewis Eliot is asked what he wants. " 'Of course, I want to see a better world.' " Pressed as to what he wants for himself, he says simply, " 'I want success. . . . I don't mean to spend my life unknown. . . . And if I fail, I shan't make any excuses. I shall say that it is my own fault.' 'Is there anything else you want?' This time I hesitated. Then I said: 'I think I want love.' " [19]

But for Lewis Eliot love does not come as a luxury after the fulfilment of ambition. Snow is a strong believer in romantic love, and Lewis Eliot while he is still a poor student falls in love with Sheila Knight, the daughter of a wealthy clergyman. Sheila is incapable of warmth in any human relation, though she continues to hope that she will fall in love or be mastered by some emotion. She is not a very satisfactory object of romantic love, but Lewis Eliot's attraction to her is as powerful as his ambition—even though he knows, and is warned by Sheila herself and by his friends, that she will hurt him. Much of *Time of Hope* is the story of Lewis Eliot's passion for Sheila. Sheila's quest, like Roy Calvert's, is vain. At last, when Lewis Eliot is beginning to succeed at the bar, she agrees to marry him, not because she loves him but because he is persistent and she trusts him. The marriage is bitterly unhappy and damages Lewis Eliot's career. Yet he cannot leave Sheila, and when at the end of the novel she has offered to leave him he tells her to stay. "It was simply that she touched the depth of my vanity and suffering, and that this was my kind of love." [20]

What underlies the two main concerns of the story, love and ambition, is possessive love. Lewis Eliot's ambition is a result partly of his mother's urging, partly of his effort to be free—of her love, and of everything but that which he makes himself. His love for Sheila comes from the same root in his character: with Sheila he can love without the burden of being loved. Even when she makes him miserable and mars his chances of success he is unable to leave her. The revelation of the roots of his action is a subtle and partial one. His ambition at first, and for a very long time, seems to be no more than the ordinary desire for success. Similarly his love for Sheila seems at first to be conventional romantic love. Only gradually does he begin to understand his love, and then only to the extent that he knows that somehow he has chosen this kind of love, that the choice comes from some flaw in his character. At the end of the novel he sees what has become of his hopes:

I had longed for a better world; and this was the summer of 1933. I had longed for fame: and I was a second-rate lawyer. I had longed for love: and I was bound for life to a woman who never had love for me and who had exhausted mine.

As I remembered, I was curiously at one with myself. . . . I had not seen enough of my life yet to perceive the full truth of what my nature needed. I could not distinguish the chance from the inevitable. But I already knew that my bondage to Sheila was no chance. Somehow I was so made that I had to reject my mother's love and all its successors. Some secret caution born of a kind of vanity made me bar my heart to any who forced their way within. I could only lose caution and vanity, bar and heart, the whole of everything I was, in the torment of loving someone like Sheila, who invaded me not at all and made me crave for a spark of feeling, who was so wrapped in herself that only the violence and suffering of such a love as mine brought the slightest glow.[21]

Homecoming, the sixth novel of the sequence, was published in 1956. It continues to fulfilment the story of Lewis Eliot and is the key book of the sequence. It is also the finest of those novels written so far, with all the unity and economy of *Time of Hope* and all of the richness and variety of the portrait gallery novels.

Homecoming takes up the story of Lewis Eliot where *Time of Hope* leaves off. Its first section covers Sheila's final breakdown and suicide. The rest of the novel deals with the dual matters of Lewis Eliot's career and his fulfilment in love. While Sheila was alive he had reconciled himself to a position as Cambridge don and consultant to an industrialist. During the War he gets a new start and rises high in one of the Ministries. (He has in fact—free of Sheila and through the circumstances of the War—become successful, although it means somewhat less to him now.) Accompanying this success is a gradual withdrawal into the role of spectator. He works hard, he is interested in his friends and is thought by them to be one of the most generous of men, unsparing of time and sympathy. But, as he comes to discover, this is once again a kind of vanity, for he is giving without receiving, he is preserving an uncommitted core of selfhood.

During this time Lewis Eliot falls in love again. Margaret is warm and responsive, in every way a contrast to Sheila. But because Lewis Eliot's love is still tainted with the old inability to yield himself fully, Margaret marries someone else. Gradually Lewis Eliot comes to understand more of himself and is finally willing to accept love. He and Margaret are married (this is rather inconvenient for her first husband, who is a decent enough person: the very strongest, if somewhat inconsistent, part of Snow's morality is his faith in romantic love). In the final section, when their child is dangerously ill, Lewis and Margaret both become sure that all of his holding back of himself is gone.

There is in *Homecoming* a fine gallery of characters, distinct and memorable. Once again, Mr. Knight the clergyman, with his indirectness, his tricks of speech; Lufkin the industrial tycoon; a celebrated and mildly eccentric art critic; Sir Hector Rose; Bevill, the old Minister; Mrs. Beauchamp, Lewis Eliot's landlady (an old standby but quite good); the complacent doctor, Margaret's first husband, who does not believe in reading the newspapers; R. S. Robinson, the tricky and engaging publisher; George Passant, the hero of *Strangers and Brothers,* who is now clearly defined and a great deal more interesting.

We have in *Homecoming* in a very assured form and with a great deal of variety the typical Snow situations: the meeting of the personnel committee; the plans and cross-conflicts of the bureaucracy. And there is the emblematic chapter entitled "Two Kinds of Business Method," which contrasts the *avant-garde* publisher, alternately flattering and tough, gallant and cynical, and the tycoon sharpening his decisions against his "no" man.

Homecoming brings together more fully and successfully than any of the other novels Snow's major concerns, love and ambition. The fulfilment in love, the new response to ambition, bring a resolution to the tensions of the preceding novels and also to the theme of "Strangers and Brothers," for Lewis Eliot in *Homecoming* becomes a brother, not a stranger. *Homecoming* offers the most complete and balanced expression of Snow's attitudes and illuminates all the other novels. In a sense *Strangers and Brothers, The Light and the Dark, Time of Hope, The New Men,* and probably *The Conscience of the Rich* and *Corridors of Power* are all stories of failure—*Homecoming* is the one novel of fulfilment.

There remain two novels to complete the series: *The Devoted,* and the final novel about Lewis Eliot. Although the series is not finished, the first nine novels give us an adequate basis for estimating the scope and achievement of the "Strangers and Brothers" sequence as a whole.

When we attempt to survey the character and dimensions of the world of "Strangers and Brothers," we might ask ourselves, as we would with any novelist whose central preoccupation is character, what kind of assumptions Snow holds about human nature. If for the sake of the exercise we were to draw up a list of these assumptions, we would find that he has a strong sense of the conflicts between overt behavior and real intention, that he feels that we have a good deal of the destructive within us along with decent and generous impulses, and that he is especially interested in characters that are tricky and complex. What this adds up to is a conventional notion of character, which has assimilated without great difficulty the heritage suggested by the names Freud and Dostoevsky. If we ask what Snow believes about the driving forces of human nature, we get answers like love, ambition, desire for power.

Snow's ideas about character are thus neither exciting nor profound. Nor does he present them as such. The very conventionality of the ideas suggests that we are to look elsewhere, to look for what he can do with such notions of character, in other words, to look for judgment, penetration, insight.

In "Strangers and Brothers," Snow presents all sorts of men, events, and institutions, and what strikes us again and again is how singularly free he is from blame, superiority, disapproval. Although people are ambitious and self-seeking, he is not ready to condemn. Our love for others is often tinged with possessiveness, but this is accepted with the observation that the Orientals call it a darkness of the heart.

In an earlier chapter I discussed this attitude as it appears in terms of public affairs; again and again on matters of the workings of Government. Snow is a great deal more concerned to understand and to judge rightly than to censure. This temper I have called worldly. In politics it is the attitude of people who are interested in improving the world by means of entering into it. It is the attitude of those who carry responsibility, of those who believe in politics rather than ideology. (It is not always easy to take account of the differences between English and American responses to Snow in this matter. Snow's pragmatism looks somewhat different in England, where it is an old story, and for many associated with compromise, inertia, and failure, and in the United States where it is, so to speak, newly discovered, and part of the equipment of sophisticated liberals.)

For the moment I should like to concentrate on this attitude as it attempts to say something about how we live, how we find some sort of fulfilment in the actual world. For Lewis Eliot the answer seems to be that we live in the world as it is, seeking fulfilment, with some limit put on self-seeking. But if we are sensitive enough, conscientious enough, as Lewis Eliot is, we must ask how do we live in the world as it is without being complacent. The test for those who take such an approach is perhaps their sense of the complexity of the problem, and in fact, of the ultimate irreconcilability of what they desire to reconcile. In the "Strangers and Brothers" sequence Snow has too much sense of the difficulty of this reconciliation to be classed with the complacent.

On the other hand he is far short of the dramatic and heroic stoicism of a Camus facing the absurd. Much of the appeal of the "Strangers and Brothers" sequence lies in the fact that Snow feels that it is possible to find some fulfilment in the modern world, that he is a man of sensibility and decent impulses, with a good deal of the largeness and generosity of the liberal humanist tradition, who asserts that it is possible to survive in the era of the Cold War and the organization world without necessarily losing one's soul.

If we put it in terms of ideas, what emerges from the history of Lewis Eliot comes to something like this. Lewis Eliot learns how to retain most of the liberal political goals without the liberal political ideology. He acknowledges what is valid in the romantic personal morality but not its glorification of failure and worship of alienation. To put it negatively, he finds out how to live without the opium of liberal political ideology or romantic personal morality.

This is no doubt a reasonable point of view. The real question about Snow's fiction, however, is not whether its attitudes should be praised as reasonable or denounced as commonplace but how well they are held, whether they remain dully sensible (a virtue in a public man but not in a novelist) or whether they are held with the vigor of mind and largeness of imagination that will transcend any question of their immediate relevance as an ethical posture. Whether these attitudes amount to trimming or to a dynamic equilibrium of tensions is, then, finally a question of art.

In the "Strangers and Brothers" series the art creates

a dialectic centering on the questions of success and failure. The dialectic on the one hand records faithfully all of the tensions in this area and on the other works out of them some adjudication and reconciliation. The process manifests itself and structures the novels in three ways: in the interaction between Lewis Eliot and the heroes whom he describes; in the use of a vast field of characters; and in the internalization of the conflict in the character and history of Lewis Eliot himself.

As for the first of these means of creating and dealing with tensions—the use of the narrator—Snow takes a series of romantic heroes, Roy Calvert, George Passant, Charles March, Martin Eliot, and presents them as seen by and in interaction with Lewis Eliot, a self-possessed, realistic, prudent man. Lewis Eliot sympathetically presents the histories of men strikingly different from himself. Out of this tension arises a series of complex evaluations and adjustments that combine sympathy and critical insight.

A second means of adjudication is provided by the large cast of characters. They are a remarkable demonstration of the relish with which Snow responds to a wide variety of temperaments. But they also constitute a field for the working out of a series of judicious balances, a vast context for the central story of Lewis Eliot, which most fully embodies the reconciliation of opposites.

If we group these characters in terms of success and failure, we have on the one hand characters who are romantics, extremists, failures—Sheila, Roy Calvert, George Passant, Charles March and his father, Martineau, Jago, Sawbridge, Mr. Knight, the younger Martin Eliot. On the other hand we have a set of worldly, successful, prudent, unromantic characters, likely to show up in positions of power: Brown, Bevill, Sir Hector Rose, the later Martin Eliot, Eden, Crawford, Sir Philip March, Osbaldiston.

Within each of the two large groups of characters, there are great variations. Thus among the men of power and responsibility, who tend to be agreeable but do not, like the romantics, "raise the emotional temperature of life," Hector Rose is competent but chilly; Arthur Brown, who has equal competence, is good company; Bevill is something of an eccentric.

The dramatic focus of the series is pretty much on the failures: Martin Eliot, Charles March, Roy Calvert, and George Passant, each is the hero of a novel (partly one suspects because Snow is concerned with arguing himself and his readers out of excessive fascination with the type; more than that, of course, because of their greater dramatic and psychological interest). In general, however, his judgment is with the people who have found some means of accommodation, who have rejected the all-or-nothing view and made the best of what must be.

The notable exception to this is Roger Quaife. He is neither a prudent administrator nor a poetic failure. He is a man for whom morality springs out of action, a man whose center is courage, conviction. (He is suggestive of the early Churchill, and Snow's article on Churchill is an instructive gloss on Roger's character.) [22] As Lewis Eliot is not without imagination, so Roger is not without judgment. But as Lewis Eliot's strength is judgment, worldly wisdom, so Roger's strength is fortitude, determination. And we are reminded in *Corridors of Power* that courage can be a better thing than principle: Rubin and Getliffe are high-principled men, but neither would have the nerve to take the chances Roger does.

Although Snow gives a certain approval to the successful, his effort is after all one of adjudication. To oversimplify: he notes the failure of the romantic figures but admires them on a personal level; he respects the competence of the worldly but notes the price that they have had to pay. (He does not present people who have sold their souls for success, though he does have something like the opposite type, the romantic who has sacrificed the world for integrity.)

This is to say that Snow does not accept as true *a priori* the disjunction between virtue and success; his characters face the problem not of choosing the side on which virtue lies, but of reconciling, achieving harmony, and trying to cut losses.

Running all through the concern with success and failure is Snow's belief in the value of self-knowledge, a sense of one's limitations, a capacity for self-doubt. Without it the romantics are merely poetic failures (Martineau) and the successful are dully competent or hustlers (Crawford or Houston Eggar). With self-knowledge a character becomes capable of reconciling opposed claims, for a large part of what we must reconcile is the conflict with the darker side of our own natures. Snow's strongest sympathy is with the kind of person " 'who knows something about himself. And is appalled. And has to forgive himself to get along.' " [23]

At the center of this large group of characters is Lewis Eliot. He is at once failure and success, and his varied career incorporates most fully and internalizes the conflicts of the series and works out a reconciliation in both public and private terms. Lewis Eliot's wide friendships and varied experiences enable him to test himself against a great variety of men and issues and to discover how to respond to the claims of power and responsibility and to the claims of individual conscience and sensibility.

Lewis Eliot's openness enables Snow to operate at his most pragmatic, taking issues one by one, dealing not with propositions but with cases. And to each case he brings all his insight, judgment, and sympathy. Take the matter of his commitment to the established management of power. In *Homecoming* he is asked to mollify a distinguished liberal who has protested against the Government's position in the atomic spy trials:

> I had not enjoyed defending the establishment: but I was also irked by the arrogance of men of decent feeling like Davidson, who had had the means to cultivate their decent feelings without the social interest or realism to imagine where they led.[24]

A few chapters later Lewis Eliot is at a committee meeting at which his friend George Passant is passed over for a civil service permanency. Lewis Eliot is angry at the strain of timidity which runs through the committee's prudence:

> The men I sat with in their offices, with their moral certainties, their comfortable, conforming indignation

which never made them put a foot out of step—they were the men who managed the world, they were the people who in any society came out on top. They had virtues denied the rest of us: I had to give them my respect. But that morning I was on the other side.[25]

For all the movement toward reconciliation, Snow has a strong sense of life as tragic—he is not complacent about suffering and evil:

> Sometimes he knew that the depths of harshness and suffering will go along with the gentle, corruption and decadence along with the noble, as long as we are men. They are as innate in the George Passants, in ourselves, as the securities and warmth upon which we build our hopes.[26]

> It was jet-clear that, despite its emollients and its joys, individual life was tragic: a man was ineluctably alone, and it was a short way to the grave. But, believing that with stoical acceptance, Martin saw no reason why social life should also be tragic: social life lay within one's power, as human loneliness and death did not.[27]

The sense of individual life as lonely, tragic, is suggested in the general title of the series—"Strangers and Brothers": one of the largest facts of man's existence is his estrangement from his fellow men and his capacity for brotherhood.

Snow has endeavored to bridge the gap between public and private concerns by applying to our situation the sensibility and technical resources of the classical English novel, with its concern for the externals of behavior, its judiciousness and moral centrality. Still, there is a subdued prophetic strain in Snow. The two major concerns of his fiction, love and power, converge in an ideal of humility. What one needs, what Lewis Eliot is so long and painfully learning, what so many of the other characters lack, is the ability to accept love, to give up the vanity of self-possession. And what one needs so that he can be trusted with power is not political or executive talent so much as humility. Given Snow's tolerance, he is fairly hard on the doctrinaire, whose pride of idea makes them dangerous, because it keeps them from seeing things as they are. The snobs, the stuffed academics, the Communists, the reformers, all lack this humility. On the other hand the men of power to whom Snow gives a certain approval—Arthur Brown, Bevill, Sir Philip March, and Lewis Eliot himself—all have a sense of their limitations, they impose no formulas on experience, and because they come to experience only with their openness they can learn from it. And this, whether it is prophecy or commonplace pragmatic observation, is at once the root and final fruit of Snow's worldliness.

4 ❧

Snow's Art

SNOW's very success in dealing with the moral and political experience of our time has diverted attention from his artistic achievement. Even his admirers have helped to crystallize the view of Snow as an intelligent and thoughtful commentator, and examinations of his fiction have tended to dwell upon his large attitudes and his sense of character. The recurring comparisons to Trollope reinforce the image of a plain novelist with unusual gifts of psychological penetration, discrimination, and tolerance, but with only mediocre gifts as an artist.

Except in the most general terms, not much has been

said, for example, about the remarkable formal economy of *Homecoming*, or about the Proustian devices of repetition of place and of involuntary memory, or about the complex structure of the "Strangers and Brothers" sequence as a whole. A good deal has been said about Snow's bridging the gap between public and private, but not much about how he does so.

Snow's own view of his art is a useful starting place. It is, like the view of any writer who feels himself in revolt against established conventions, somewhat polemical and at times extreme. He has been emphatic in asserting that the kind of fiction we have been calling modern is exhausted, and he sees himself as a spokesman for "a new tide of realistic and humanistic writing." [1] Whether or not there is such a tide, Snow's statements have been used against him to prove that he is a graceless or resourceless writer, lamely perpetuating the Trollope or Galsworthy tradition.

The development of Snow's fiction makes it clear that his decision as to what kind of novel to write is not haphazard and that he is not insensible to the fiction of the twentieth century. His experiments with the detective story and the science fiction work, and the various shifts in direction in *The Search* and the first few novels of the "Strangers and Brothers" series show pretty clearly that Snow was trying to find the kind of instrument suited to his temper and vision. As he has said, he is one of those writers who have had to "nose their way."

The view that Snow has not "contributed anything to the novel," that is, made any distinctive technical innovations, is irrelevant except in terms of some dubious evolutionary view of art. The relevant question is whether the means he has chosen are suited to what he has to say and whether he says it well with those means.

According to Snow's own statement, he has turned away from the material and methods which are associated with the remarkable development of fiction in the first three decades of this century: the intensive exploration of individual sensibility, particularly through stream of consciousness; the extensive use of symbolism and irony, and the heavy emphasis on the verbal texture of fiction; and in general the development of the techniques of obliquity and indirection.

One of the characteristic achievements of the twentieth-century novel has been, to use D. H. Lawrence's phrase, "putting all the action inside." The accomplishments of this kind of fiction are now matters of history, beyond serious debate. But after forty years or so writers and critics are in something of a revisionist mood about the view that this is the sovereign method for dealing with experience. The poetry of Proust and Joyce remains supreme, but in lesser hands the wholly internalized drama of the psyche runs the risk of becoming dull. With little action and without the operation of the reflective intelligence, the history of a sensibility can easily become a narcissistic mumble. Snow has said that "this kind of novel-writing [Joyce's and Virginia Woolf's, two of Snow's villains] dominated a good deal of sensibility in England for a generation. It has ceased to do so. To be brief and curt, no serious novelist under fifty could now conceivably contemplate writing a novel in this genre . . . such novels are as dead as *dada*." [2]

[87]

Snow's objections to the novel of sensibility have caused a good deal of confusion. A number of critics have expressed surprise that he complains about sensibility when he seems to share the English novel's traditional obsessive concern with personal relations.[3] What Snow has not made completely clear in his statements is that his objection is not to the concern with personal relations but to the minute examination of sensibility in isolation and to the divorce of personal relations from morality and public affairs.

The English novel, Snow says:

> has shown, from about 1915 to the present, a remarkable and ultimately suicidal tendency to narrow its range. . . . [It lacks] not the insight which tells us what it is like to be in a certain mood (at which the Americans and English have been pretty good), but the insight which probes beneath the continuum of feeling and asks, "Why should I, of all people, have this mood at all? be driven by these motives? be capable of this action? live this unique life?" This causal insight, in both Tolstoy and Dostoevsky, though in different fashions, makes for a complex and enriching interaction between their individual personages and their immense social range. It is probable, I think, that such an insight is inextricably linked with an active insight into society.[4]

In Snow's fiction this means character but not sensibility, character analysis but not stream of consciousness. There are no shimmering and elusive moments of consciousness, but rather a more traditional humanistic

view of character and motive. Snow tends to the lucid
and direct, qualities in large part provided by the use of
a narrator, who can be thought of as representing not
experience but the understanding of experience. Snow's
sense of character is large enough to accommodate complexity and unconscious motivation, but he is not interested in presenting consciousness as direct experience.

Snow explores character in his own way—by relating
it directly to plot, by making use of a reflective narrator,
by dealing with the psyche as it manifests itself in external action, by relating it to public concerns, in short by
a more social, objective, and public approach to character. And in doing this Snow has bound together the
public and the private, social fact and character. (It is
often said that Snow has gone back to Trollope, but he
is probably closer to the long and relatively unbroken
Continental tradition—Tolstoy, Manzoni, Sienkiewicz,
Undset, Martin du Gard, Sholokhov, Bacchelli—which
has always been strongly realistic and has always concerned itself with relating the public and the private.) [5]

Snow's art is a direct daylight one, one that works by
statement rather than implication; one that is straightforward rather than oblique; one that makes use of
much analysis and comment by the first person narrator.
And whatever may be said about its fashionableness, it is
hard to see how Snow, given his temperament and general direction, could have found his way to anything but
this kind of art.

One of the key ideas in Snow's non-fiction is "seeing
clearly." "It is important that we should get an under-

standing of what our managers are like and how their society works. It is important we should if the world is to be livable in." [6] Elsewhere, Snow says:

> The kind of politics in which I have been interested as a theme is, in principle, more general than Trollope's. If I have to define it in pompous and abstract terms, I should say it was the power-relations of men in organized society. This seems to me an interesting theme in itself, and obviously an important one, since these power-relations determine so much of our working lives. In fact, if I were seeking a practical reason for trying to express this theme in terms of art, I should repeat what I have said elsewhere—you've got to understand how the world ticks, if you're going to have any chance of making it tick better.[7]

The point that Snow regularly stresses is that our vision should be clear, free from illusion. In his article "The Corridors of Power" he talks about something like Bacon's idols of the theatre, that is, the dramatized version of reality that keeps us from knowing what is. For Snow the "idol" is the romantic view of men of power as conspirators:

> Those pictures seem to be made up of all the secret societies, all the grey eminences, we have ever heard of: Lenin's sealed train, the atomic spies, Harry Hopkins at the White House, the Yalta Conference—such pictures can be exciting, they may even be true, but they do not make it easier to understand the world we are living in. The working truth is a good deal more difficult, nothing like as lurid, and quite as interesting.[8]

That is a realist's credo, and most readers of Snow will agree that the realistic account of how power works is as interesting as it may be useful.

In his concern for understanding the world about him, Snow has many affinities with the older English novelists—Fielding, Jane Austen, George Eliot, Thackeray, Trollope. Theirs is a vision that is central, equable, wide-ranging, concerned with seeing things free of eccentric perspective or extravagance. Typically they employ realism, a plain style, generally a fair-sized cast of characters, and often overlapping and multiple presentations of the same matter. Theirs is, in short, a horizontal view of reality. They are surer about particulars than about general truths and like to let larger truths emerge from the examination of many cases: even then they are reluctant to state these truths in propositions. Their aim is understanding rather than prophecy or the poetry of consciousness.

As with the other novelists in this tradition, plot is more than a necessary evil for Snow in the "Strangers and Brothers" sequence. Theme and character are explicitly manifested in action: a marriage, a divorce, the rejection of a job, a plan, a piece of business, the choice of a career. This kind of external action not only provides a strong focus for character and theme but also enables Snow to deal with a wide range of public matters, to explore how a Whitehall department works, how a college goes about electing a Master, what kind of choice the scientists making the atomic bomb had, and so on.

Ordinarily, in novels so much concerned with character and so strong on analysis, even the most intelligent comment (as in Proust) begins to bog down and to make for dull or at best slow reading. As I suggested earlier, Snow's solution, evolved after the troubles of *Strangers and Brothers,* has been a strong what-happens-next plot: will George get the job? will Jago get elected? will the atomic pile work?

Trollope described plot as merely a vehicle which is necessary for the real concern—the passengers. In *The Last Chronicle of Barset,* for example, the question, "Did Mr. Crawley steal the check?", is nearly a joke, a joke that lasts for eight hundred pages while Trollope makes a remarkable exploration of Mr. Crawley's character. But in Snow's novels—certainly after *The Light and the Dark*—the suspense is created by character and gives rise to further questions about character. In *The Masters*—which in terms of plot is a *tour de force*—we want to know whether the more sympathetic character will get elected; that question is answerable only in terms of a number of lesser questions: whether Nightingale will vote out of resentment or out of self-interest, whether Pilbrow will vote in terms of his political conscience or of his sense of the worth of his friends. And so on, into the analysis of almost every one of the fellows, and of the interaction of the fellows as plans and counter-plans develop. Thus the analysis of character and of the workings of the group is not simply strung on the question of the election but is the means of moving the action forward, of raising problems and answering them. And this, which is true of *The Masters,* a novel without a theme or a central character, and of the simi-

larly structured *Affair,* is all the more true of the novels
with central themes or main characters, *The New Men,
The Conscience of the Rich, Time of Hope,* and *Homecoming.*

Even more than plot, style is characteristic of Snow's
way of looking at the world. It is also one of the most
common grounds of complaint about Snow. His style is
said to be flat, alkaline, prosy. It is true that Snow is not
what is commonly recognized as a stylist—that is, his
style has no marked or unusual characteristics. Most of
the comments about flatness, however, are based on a
failure to recognize the function of style and on the
assumption that all writing ought to have certain qualities of imaginativeness, vividness, brightness.

Snow has chosen a direct style because it is essential to
the way he looks at things. His art is one of the declara-
tive sentence. He is unusually sparing of metaphor. He
has little interest in the standard description of what
people wore, of what color the curtains were. He is concerned with character and the interaction of characters;
when there is description it is subordinated to this. He
has, indeed, his own poetry of exclusion. A short passage
from *The Light and the Dark* gives us an example of
how Snow even at his most lyrical keeps description sub-
ordinate:

> I smelt blossom everywhere as I walked through the
> town that afternoon. The sky was bright, cloudless
> and pale, and the wind cut coldly down the narrow
> Cambridge streets. Round Fenner's the trees flared
> out in bloom, and the scent was sweet, heady and
> charged with one's desires.

As soon as he has presented the Cambridge weather and landscape, one of the recurring motifs of the novel, Snow shifts to character:

> I had been walking all the afternoon weighed down by a trouble. It was a trouble I was used to, there was no help for it, it could only be endured. It gnawed acutely that day, and so I had tried to comfort myself, walking alone.[9]

Similarly, *Homecoming* opens with a paragraph of description—a passage of great thematic import both for this novel and for the series as a whole:

> It was a February afternoon of smoky sunshine, as I walked down along the embankment to my wife. The river ran white in the sun, the plume from a tug's funnel came out blue as cigarette-smoke; on the far bank the reflections from windows shone through haze, and down towards Chelsea where I was walking, the smoke was so thick that the skyline, the high chimneys, had smudged themselves into it.

The evocative and symbolic elements of the scene are deliberately underplayed, and Snow moves immediately to the psychological:

> The day was a Tuesday, the year 1938; I had not been home since the Thursday before, which was my usual routine, as I had to spend half my week in Cambridge. I felt an edge of anxiety, a tightness of the nerves, as I always did going home after an absence, even an absence as short as this. Ever since I could remember, seeking deep into my childhood, I had felt this dread on the way home, this dread of what might be waiting for me.

It was nothing serious, it was just one of the reasonless anxieties one had to live with, it was no worse
than that. Even now, when sometimes it turned out
not so reasonless, I had got used to it. On those Tues-
day evenings, walking home from Millbank to Chelsea
along the river, I was anxious as I always had been,
returning home, but I had put out of mind the special
reason why.[10]

Since sensory description is so little important in
Snow (though it is not so unimportant as in Jane
Austen), we must look at Snow's style to see how it is
used in the presentation of character and situation—
what does Snow do with such a leaned-down functional
style?

I intruded so far as to tell Charles that he ought to
forget the night of the concert, and meet his father
more than half-way. Charles himself was happy in the
prospect of his marriage, which was fixed for three
months ahead. He was also gratified that he could
discipline himself enough to work patiently at his
medicine; he had done it for a year, and he had no
misgivings left. So that he was ready to listen to everything I said. His natural kindness, his deep feeling for
his father now shone out. He wanted Mr. March to be
happy for the rest of his life. He would respond to any
overture his father made. I tried to persuade him to go
to his father, on his own initiative, and ask to be made
independent.[11]

Beyond a certain compression, nothing particularly dis-
tinguishes this passage—it is clear, and adequate for its
somewhat limited intentions. On the other hand, there

are passages in which it is immediately evident that Snow achieves a great deal more than the straightforward *résumé* of events:

Thus he plunged among twenty-five years of marriage—not at all tranquil years, because he could not be tranquil anywhere, but full of the life he wanted and in which he breathed his native air. He was passionately fond of his wife, and he was occupied with plenty of excitements, major and minor; the major excitements about his children as they grew up, and the minor ones of his fortune, Bryanston Square, Haslingfield, the servants, the whole economico-personal system of which he was the core.

He had not been bored. He had enjoyed his life. He still enjoyed it. He would have taken it over again on the same terms, and gone through it with as much zest.

And yet, it was foreign to his nature not to be frank with himself, and he felt that he had paid a price. Underneath this life which suited him, which soaked up the violence underneath and let him become luxuriantly himself, he knew that he had lost some self-respect. He had been happier than most men, but it meant that he chose to run away from the contest.

Even Mr. March, the most realistic of men, could not always forgive himself for his own nature. He could not quite forget the illusion, which we all have, most strongly when we are young, that every kind of action is possible to us if only we use our will. He felt as we all do, when we have slowly come to terms with our temperament and no longer try to be different from ourselves: we may be happier now, but we cannot help looking back to the days when we struggled against the sight of our limitations, when, miserable and conflict-ridden perhaps, we still in flashes of hope held the whole world in our hands. For the loss, as we come to know ourselves, is that now we know what we can never do.[12]

The rhythmic effects, the use of climax in the first paragraph, the emphasis achieved by the series of simple sentences in the second paragraph, and the overall working out of balance and antithesis toward the final climactic generalization—all these make the passage a great deal more than the plain prose of communication.

Some of Snow's characteristic stylistic devices—which are basic to his conception and presentation of character—can be isolated in a passage which occurs in the early pages of *The Masters*. At first it appears that Snow is simply giving the essential facts about Jago, methodically going through the details of physical appearance and then enumerating aspects of character:

He [Jago] apologised for disturbing me. He apologised too much, for a man who was often so easy.

But sometimes he found the first moments of a meeting difficult; that was true with everyone he met, certainly with me, though we liked each other. I had got used to his excessive apologies and his over-cordial greetings. He made them that night, though he was excited, though he was grave and tense with his news.

He was a man of fifty, and some, seeing that he had gone both bald and grey, thought he looked older. But the first physical impression was deceptive. He was tall and thick about the body, with something of a paunch, but he was also small-boned, active, light on his feet. In the same way, his head was massive, his forehead high and broad between the fringes of fair hair; but no one's face changed its expression quicker, and his smile was brilliant. Behind the thick lenses, his eyes were small and intensely bright, the eyes of a young and lively man. At a first glance, people might think he looked a senator. It did not take them long to discover how mercurial he was. His temper was as quick as his smile; in everything he did his nerves seemed on the surface. In fact, people forgot all about the senator and began to complain that sympathy and emotion flowed too easily. Many of them disliked his love of display. Yet they were affected by the depth of his feeling. Nearly everyone recognised that, though it took some insight to perceive that he was not only a man of deep feeling, but also one of passionate pride.[13]

Snow's characters are almost always interesting, and Snow is remarkably judicious in presenting them. What is evident in this passage is how closely related these two qualities are. Essentially the description proceeds by working out a set of contrasts in the character. He apologized but was often easy; he apologized though he was excited; he seemed older than fifty but his appearance was deceptive; he looked a senator but one found he was really mercurial; many disliked his love of display but they were affected by his depth of feeling; everyone saw his feeling but only some his pride. Syntactically the passage depends on its series of "thoughs" and "buts." The effect is on the one hand to create the fascination of conflict and contradiction, and on the other to give us a sense of a judicious appraisal of the complexity of the man. Both in syntax and overall effects the passage has affinities with the general process of reconciliation and balance in Snow. There are the appearances, which are true enough, and the realities, which are more deeply true—the showy and the genuine, the warm and the awkward, the senator and the mercurial man. At the same time there is a great deal of the qualification that indicates Snow's reluctance to over-simplify, that makes him seem so judicious. Snow's strategy is to hold in proper proportion the appearance and the reality, the major assertions and the minor qualifications, and to keep all of them before us simultaneously.

We get something of the same method in Snow's famous group and committee scenes, in which he scrutinizes a variety of characters and the interaction among them. The following is typical. We have just been told that the narrator and two other fellows have been having a glass of port and listening to the views of Crawford on science, on the Royal Society, on the revolution in technology:

> Crawford enjoyed talking; some were put off by his manner and could not bear to listen, but they lost something. He had not the acute penetrating intellect of Roy Calvert; in an intelligence test he would not have come out as high as, say, the Master or Winslow; and he had no human insight at all. But he had a broad, strong, powerful mind, not specially apt for entertaining but made to wear.
>
> Nightingale sat outside the little circle of three round which the bottle passed. Since he learned the news, his expression was still taut with strain, but his eyes had become bright and fierce. There was nothing

crushed about him; his whole manner was active, harsh, and determined as he listened to Crawford. He listened without speaking. He did not once give his envious smile. But, once as I watched him, his eyes left Crawford for an instant and stared inimically at mine. They were feverishly bright.[14]

A careful examination of Snow's style shows that its major virtue is not the absence of distortion, the "dry light"; rather its strength is in its precision in rendering character and situation as full of contrast and yet intelligible:

Bevill was an aristocrat; he had an impersonal regard for big business, but in his heart rarely liked the company of a business man. In Lufkin's presence, as in the presence of most others of the human race, Bevill could sound matey; he was not feeling so, he wanted to keep on amiable terms because that was the general principle of his life, but in fact he longed to bolt off to his club. While Lufkin, who had made his way by scholarships and joined his firm at seventeen, felt for politicians like Bevill something between envy and contempt, only softened by a successful man's respect for others' success.[15]

Probably in this passage the device of antithesis is overworked. We can almost sense Snow building up to the "but in fact."

Sometimes the qualification and contrast are simply a means of arriving at precision of judgment:

Martin smiled. For himself, he would have been glad of a breathing space, to luxuriate in the success; to him, it was real success, the first he had had. But then Martin, less humble than Luke as a man, was far more so as a scientist. Luke knew his powers; he knew that this project had not stretched them; it had tested his character, but in terms of scientific imagination, it had needed little. He did not take much pride in the achievement; this was no place to rest; with all his energies, he wanted to push on.[16]

So far I have not touched on the crucial matters of tone and attitude. To see more exactly what Snow's style can do and how it works, and to see the point at which it is the instrument of his tolerance, I should like to examine a passage from *The New Men*. It occurs at a moment when the narrator is trying to dissuade his brother, a scientist in the bomb project, from writing a letter of protest which will ruin his career:

As I began to make the first opposing moves, which he was already expecting, I was thinking, his was a letter which an able man only writes when he is near breaking point. Only his mask was stoical, as he sat there, his fingers spread like a starfish on the arms of his chair. In his letter—whatever he had written I should be trying to suppress it—he had not made the best of his case. Yet I agreed with him in all that mattered. Looking back years later, I still agreed with him.

I felt it so, that afternoon, when I set myself to make Martin keep quiet. I shut away the sense of outrage, my own sense of outrage as well as his, and brought out the worldly wise, official's arguments, such as we had displayed at Barford in July, such as he had used himself. It was not worth while making gestures for no result. One such gesture was all you were allowed; you ought to choose a time when it could do good. We had found ourselves in responsible positions; we could not give them up overnight; for everyone's sake we had to get through the next few years without a war; then one could make gestures.

There was something in what I said, but they were not the reasons, they were nowhere near the reasons, why I was calling on each ounce of nature that I possessed to force him to conform. It was, in fact, incomparably more simple. For a brother as for a son, one's concern is, in the long run, prosaic and crude. One is anxious about their making a living; one longs for their success, but one wants it to be success as the world knows it, reputation among solid men. For myself, my own "respectable" ambitions had damped down by now, I should perhaps have been able, if the choice was sharp enough, to throw them away and face a scandal. For myself; but not for him.

I had seen friends throw away what most men clung to, respectability, money, fame. Roy Calvert: Charles March: even old Martineau. I understood why they had done it, I should have been the last to dissuade them. But they were friends, and Martin was a brother. The last thing you want with a brother is that he should fulfil a poetic destiny.[17]

This passage is one of the high points of *The New Men*, its subject, possessive love, one of the major themes of the "Strangers and Brothers" sequence, and the conflict is important for the narrator as well as for his brother.

One of the first things we notice is the effect of distancing, of impartiality, fairness. "Opposing moves, which he was already expecting" suggests the narrator detached and able to see the quarrel with his brother as a part of a pattern. The laconic quality of "I set myself to make Martin keep quiet" and the matter-of-fact notation of the narrator's "outrage" again suggest distancing and impartiality. And of course there is the obvious effect of "looking back years later." But in the last paragraph the balance and detachment begin to yield. The narrator is not perturbed; he understands, he even sympathizes, but he does not ultimately approve of his brother's choice, it would be a "poetic destiny." The control of tone is impressive as it moves from the dismissive "what most men clung to" down at last to "poetic destiny." It is in just such passages that Snow manages what I have called the art of balance, in which through a blending of distance and engagement he gives us the sense of judiciousness and breadth.

There is, however, another and perhaps more important set of effects operating in the passage. There is a carefully controlled shifting back and forth between the particular and dramatic on the one hand and the general and reflective on the other. The effect is to give the passage a largeness that a purely dramatic scene cannot have, to bring about an interplay between drama and the reflective intelligence. Speaking of novelists who suppress half of what they know in order to write novels, Snow says, "When not dressed in their novelists' uniforms, they often have good intellects. But they feel, as though impelled by some bizarre code of manners, that their first duty as novelists is to divest themselves of any sign of those intellects." Snow's alternative involves a particular fusion of the investigatory, reflective and moral intelligences that specially fits the novel, and which is still the only way open to us of exploring certain aspects, including the most important aspects, of the individual and social condition. It is the elements of experience which those kinds of intelligence give—not only the here-and-now experience, but the experience of thinking about it—that we have to organise into a work of art.[18]

The phrase *"experience* of thinking about it" helps to make clear the difference between Snow's first person narrator making comments and the nineteenth-century novelist making comments in his role of omniscient author. The second, while it makes use of the reflective intelligence (as in George Eliot), is never meant as anything but reflection. Snow on the other hand, like Proust, means his narrator's observations to be an experience of thinking. The narrator does not announce a truth which he has known all along and now sees to be applicable, rather he is involved in a process of discovering, in which he is thinking things through.

The experience of thinking comes in, then, through the back-and-forth movement between dramatic reporting and reflection on the part of the narrator. The very first sentence of the passage which we have been examining begins with dramatic reporting, "As I began to make the first opposing moves, which he was already expecting," and then it shifts into reflection, "I was thinking, his was a letter which an able man only writes when he is near breaking point." The passage returns to dramatic reporting—"only his mask was stoical"—for several lines; then the narrator reflects on his own conduct—and the reflection appears to take place as he writes—"There was something in what I had said, but they were not the reasons, they were nowhere near the reasons. . . . It was, in fact, incomparably more simple. For a brother as for a son, one's concern is, in the long run, prosaic and crude." We have already begun a shift towards generalization in the "one," a shift further developed in the next sentence, "One is anxious. . . ." But we do not stay long on the plane of general reflection; immediately the narrator turns to a personal response, talking about his own success and the intensity of his feeling for his brother. Having reflected on possessive love, the narrator recalls the experience of his friends—again moving toward the general—then pulls up with, "But they were friends, and Martin was a brother," and concludes the passage with a statement that combines all of the force of the particular and the general: "The last thing you want with a brother is that he should fulfil a poetic destiny."

A particularly complex passage such as this illustrates almost all of the strengths in Snow's style—the sophisticated use of reflection and generalization and the careful control of tone. Very often this method can be used to produce an effect of discovery:

> Myself, I believed that Martin had two motives. The nearer one was to him, the more often he seemed hard, selfish, cautious, calculating. . . . I was pretty sure that the rumours about him were right, that he had not been able to resist working out the combinations for the next magisterial election. I was pretty

sure that he had decided it was worth trying for Brown as Master, so that if it came off, he could walk into the Senior Tutorship himself.

That was all true. But it was not all. There was something else within him which made him a more interesting man. At its roots it might not be more amiable than those other roots which made him a hard self-seeker; but it certainly made him more surprising and more capable of good. It was something like a curious kind of self-regard. He knew as well as anyone else that he was hard, selfish, obsessively careful: but he knew, what no one else did, that he had sometimes wanted to be different from that. . . .

Now he was doing it again . . . out of that special kind of self-regard, tinged with and disentangleable from his feeling that he had to be responsible. . . .

That was one motive. The other, it seemed to me, was much simpler. Martin was a natural politician. . . . If anyone could take it through to success, Martin could. . . . Martin enjoyed using his political skills. As a rule, he had used them for his own purposes. . . . It was a treat for him—and I believed that unless one understood that, one didn't understand him or other worldly men—to think of using them for a purpose which he felt, without any subtlety or complexity at all, to be nothing but good.[19]

The rhetoric of this passage is essentially that of discovery and surprise. The extraordinary thing is that the discovery purports to be made by a successful, knowledgeable, middle-aged man who is talking about his own brother. And this points to what is probably one of the

secrets of Snow's power as a novelist—a sense of wonder.
For all his worldliness, Snow has a kind of innocence, a
capacity for surprise and awe—about how colleges work,
about how bureaucracies grow, but mostly about people. He never seems to know in advance that systems are
corrupt or benevolent, that human nature is hopelessly
selfish, or predictably ambivalent. Snow writes as
though he is making discoveries. Lewis Eliot is in and of
the world, but he sees it in an almost childlike way—free
of preconception, unconcerned with blaming, fascinated
by everything that goes on. In this fascination with the
variousness and complexity of character, Snow is very
different from a "studier of character" like Jane Austen,
who has high and fixed notions of conduct against which
she measures behavior. Snow judges, of course, but in a
most tolerant way, and interest and curiosity are
stronger than judgment:

> In my youth I had been as tempted as most men by
> the petty treachery, the piece of malice warm on the
> tongue at a friend's expense, the kind of personal im-
> perialism . . . in which one imposes oneself upon
> another. Even more I had been fascinated by the same
> quicksands in other men. As to many of us when young,
> the labile, the shifting, the ambivalent, the Lebedevs
> and the Fyodor Karamazovs, had given me an intima-
> tion of the depth and wonder of life.[20]

To return to the particulars of Snow's style, while his
use of reflection and generalization is often dramatic,
subtle, modulated, it can have also an epigrammatic
quality. The range of comments (whether they report
Lewis Eliot thinking and discovering on the spot or sim-

ply reflecting after the event as he writes a novel) is surprisingly narrow, and suggests a deliberately restricted focus. They hardly ever refer to topical matters or to immediate political problems. Almost all of them are psychological observations—on worldliness and simplicity, on ambition, on realists, on vanity and self-esteem, and particularly on the workings of power: who gets trusted by a committee; how obtuse people get their way where cleverer men fail; how conflict affects the combatants.

Such reflection has to avoid on the one hand offensive superiority and on the other utter banality. Inevitably, since the reader must accept a statement as true, there is a tendency toward the familiar and obvious. This may be a source of the complaint that Snow deals in clichés, though on the whole the complaint seems unjustified. A sample will give some idea of the quality of these comments:

> Like many brave men, they did not bear a grudge against the timid. But, like many ill men, they resented the well.[21]

> Nearly always, I thought, there was something men or women were protecting, when deliberately, and with pride, almost with conceit, they showed you their most callous side.[22]

> Nightingale smiled, with the dreadful suspiciousness of the unworldly.[23]

> For his relation with the Master had nothing of the strain that comes between a protégé and his patron—where all emotion is ambivalent, unless both parties are magnanimous beyond the human limits.[24]

Men of affairs weren't sprinters: they weren't tied to
the clock: if you hurried them when they didn't pro-
pose to be hurried, you were not one of them.[25]

A more complex and very characteristic kind of reflection is the one that asserts an appearance and then moves
to a reality:

People often thought that those who "handled"
others, "managers" of Martin's kind, were passionless.
They would have been no good at their job if they
were. No, what made them effective was that they
were capable of being infuriated on the one hand,
and managerial on the other.[26]

To move from the details of Snow's art to the "Strangers and Brothers" sequence as a whole, it is clear why
the form of a series is attractive to Snow. His concern
with balance and his treatment of large themes such as
possessive love are in the nature of things more suitable
for an extensive than an intensive presentation. Tradi-
tionally, the realistic novel has employed a wide variety
of characters and situations and often developed double
or even multiple plots in order to present its theme
fully. It has tended to present its heroes in terms of
several thematic concerns and to see its characters in as
many perspectives as possible. Snow does both of these
on a very large scale. Possessive love, for example, is
central to both of the Lewis Eliot novels; it recurs in
The New Men as a secondary theme and in *The Conscience of the Rich* as a major theme. On the other
hand, an incident such as the trial of George Passant is
presented once as dramatic climax in *Strangers and*

Brothers, of which George is the hero, and again as an episode in *Time of Hope,* where the focus is on Lewis Eliot's career as barrister. Lewis Eliot's relations with his mother are connected with ambition in *Time of Hope,* but in *Homecoming* we discover that they are central to his whole character, which must be understood in terms of possessive love.

As a novelist who has no overriding idea, who is sceptical and worldly, commonsensical, fond of individual cases, Snow is drawn to extend more and more the practice of repetition and variation. Like the law working out precedents, seeing its way through particulars, he seems to want as wide a field as possible for the exploration of his themes. While there is in the series a unified vision of the central matters of ambition and love, Snow's method is that of the fox rather than the hedgehog—"The fox knows many things, but the hedgehog knows one big thing." [27]

Although the relative importance of plot, the directness of the style, and the vast pattern of repetition and variation are in the tradition of realism, there is another element in Snow's art. He has disclaimed any attempt at direct imitation of Proust, but there are at least two areas in which he seems to have taken a hint from Proust. The first is the use of rhythmic repetition.

In the "Strangers and Brothers" series, especially in *Homecoming,* Snow makes use of the device of repetition of places and situations. The most notable is the image of homecoming, which runs through *Time of Hope* and *Homecoming.* The opening of *Time of Hope*

presents the narrator as a child coming home in the
evening with a feeling of objectless apprehension. Later
in the novel we are reminded of this opening, as we see
references to the narrator's returning home after he
takes his examinations and after he is unhappily married. The same image dominates the opening chapter of
Homecoming and is repeated throughout the book, most
strikingly at its conclusion:

> We were in sight of home. A light was shining in
> one room: the others stood black, eyeless, in the
> leaden light. It was a homecoming such as, for years, I
> thought I was not to know. Often in my childhood, I
> had felt dread as I came near home. It had been worse
> when I went, as a young man, towards the Chelsea
> house. Now, walking with Margaret, that dread had
> gone. In sight of home my steps began to quicken, I
> should soon be there with her.
>
> It was a homecoming such as I had imagined when I
> was lonely, but as one happening to others, not to
> me.[28]

Elsewhere there is this kind of binding together of
experience, often through involuntary recall. "This was
the identical train I used to catch, going home from
London after eating dinners at the Inn." [29] "For, looking into those windows from the car, I had not dared to
think of another evening when I had dined out without
my wife." [30] And running throughout the series there
are key images which acquire rich emotional overtones—
the light in the window, the view out of the window, the
walk in the park. Such images, of course, do not as in

Proust organize or dominate the novels. They simply create smaller resonances within a given novel and within the sequence as a whole.

The large structure of the series also owes something to Proust. In the same paragraph in which he disclaims imitation of Proust, Snow says that, "I myself have spent a number of years using a thematic system to organise a fair mass of material." [31] In his "Author's Note" preceding the English edition of *The Conscience of the Rich*, Snow offers an account of the sequence:

> The inner design . . . consists of a resonance between what Lewis Eliot sees and what he feels. Some of the more important emotional themes he observes through others' experience, and then finds them enter into his own. . . . The theme of possessive love is introduced through Mr. March's relation to his son: this theme reappears in *The New Men* in Lewis's own experience, through his relation to his brother, and again, still more directly, in *Homecoming*.[32]

William Cooper has explained resonance more fully:

> It is the phenomenon of something that vibrates being able to stir and magnify a similar vibration in something that has been previously *attuned*, which gives *Strangers and Brothers* its power, through evocation and revelation, over one's emotions and one's imagination.[33]

This resonance helps to structure the "Strangers and Brothers" sequence as a whole. Cooper gives a useful diagram of the groupings of the novels [34] (later works are added).

NOVELS OF OBSERVED EXPERIENCE		NOVELS OF DIRECT EXPERIENCE	
Strangers and Brothers	1925–33		
The Conscience of the Rich	1927–36	*Time of Hope*	1914–33
The Light and the Dark	1935–43		
The Masters	1937		
The New Men	1939–46	*Homecoming*	1938–48
The Affair	1953–54	*[Another novel about*	
Corridors of Power	1955–59	*Lewis Eliot]*	
[The Devoted]	1945–47		

Thus there are three cycles, each covering a stage of Lewis Eliot's life—youth, early maturity, and middle age. Within the time span of each cycle, Lewis Eliot is once the protagonist of a novel and two or three times the observer and narrator.

This grouping of the novels, however, ought to be taken loosely and suggestively. The parallelism is not worked out in detail, and there are other resonances operating through the series.

With *Corridors of Power* it becomes clear how much and how well the series renders the effects of time upon the characters (one wonders if Snow is thinking of *War and Peace*). It has always been apparent that Snow wants to register the feel of different times and the impact of historical events on men's lives. As the series nears completion it becomes clear that this is connected with the interaction between historical epochs, the aging of the characters, and the problems of power, ambition, and so on.

The account of power, we now see, is not simply dialectical but chronological. The early novels present young men just outside or on the fringes of power, hopeful, a bit envious, some of them on the way up. Later the same characters are themselves wielding power, still hoping to do better than their elders but finding it not so easy. Now in the third stage (begun in *The Affair*) Lewis Eliot and his friends (Getliffe, Rose, Osbaldiston) have had power for a long time; they are growing older, and not necessarily much wiser, a little weary and stuffy.

Quite aside from power, the characters are simply growing older, becoming a bit testy, somewhat less buoyant. Earlier we have seen men like Jago and Mr. March, for whom growing older means recognizing more clearly what one cannot do or be. Now we are beginning to see this more nearly from the inside and see it happen to those whom we remember as having been young in the earlier novels. Hector Rose, the ideal civil servant, is now the man who lives in the awareness that he will retire soon and that he has been passed over for the very top jobs. Francis Getliffe, whose angularities were earlier part of his scrupulous fairness, is now difficult, a trifle priggish, less interested in the rest of the world. All of them seem to be withdrawing somewhat, investing more of their hopes in their children.

There are still other ways in which the novels fit together into a whole so that each novel gains meaning from its place in the larger context and in turn adds meaning to the rest of the series. Thus *The Masters,* which is by itself something of a *tour de force,* is in terms of the series important for the way in which it studies the workings of power. Its analysis of a relatively isolated small group prepares us for the analysis of the somewhat larger and more influential group of scientists and bureaucrats in *The New Men* and *Homecoming,* and finally for the study of high government circles in *Corridors of Power.* To pursue the matter in another way, Lewis Eliot, whose history is central to the "Strangers and Brothers" sequence, learns about power at Cambridge, where he is observer as much as participant, more closely when he acts as liaison between bureaucrats and scientists in *The New Men,* and most fully in *Homecoming* and *Corridors of Power* where his influence is considerable and his personal involvement largest. Any one of the individual histories—Lewis Eliot, Roy Calvert, George Passant, Martin Eliot, Charles March, Roger Quaife—becomes more satisfying and meaningful when we see it in the light of all the others. When the series has been completed and the relationships which have been emerging over the years all become clear, it may well be difficult to think of "Strangers and Brothers" as anything but a single undertaking.

5 ᏸᕀ

Other Writings

ALTHOUGH *The Two Cultures* and *Science and Government* have created a great deal of controversy and have added to Snow's fame, his non-fiction is not in the long run going to affect the judgment upon his achievement as a novelist. Whatever the value of the non-fiction works, they are on the whole practical and short-term contributions to practical problems, and it is a mistake to regard them in any other way.

During the thirty years that he has been writing novels, Snow has regularly published short pieces of prose. The earlier pieces of popular scientific exposition were, one supposes, written chiefly for money. Others, such as

"Challenge to the Intellect" and "The English Realistic Novel," have been written as apologia and rationale for Snow's fiction. The most important group are what might be described as a responsible citizen's contribution to the practical problems of our society. In all his non-fiction Snow's prose is direct and is relatively free of irony or eloquence; it is, and is meant to be, communication.

During the nineteen-thirties, when he was publishing scientific papers and writing his first novels, Snow did a good many more or less popular scientific articles, such as "Science of the Year," "Controlling Reproduction," "Enjoyment of Science," "False Alarm in Physics," "Superfluity of Particles," and "What We Need from Applied Science." The pieces are informational, the tone is recognizably Snow's, and the writing is distinguished chiefly by its clarity. A good many of them convey a sense of the excitement of the Elizabethan age of physics and in general a sense of the relevance of science to the larger problems of our culture.

Snow seems to have done little miscellaneous writing during the later thirties and the first half of the forties. One of the few pieces published during these years is an article on "Careers" in *The Political Quarterly*, which reflects his concern with the problems of recruitment and resources in manpower. Since the War Snow has been writing a good deal about the larger aspects of science and of public affairs—"Moral Unneutrality of Science," "Men of Fission," "Reflections on Mr. Dean's Report," "The Corridors of Power," and so on.

Along the way he has written, again mostly since the

War, a number of pieces on literary topics with the general intent of explaining his own practice. These have frequently involved attacks on the tradition which Snow has rejected—as in "Challenge to the Intellect," and "Science, Politics, and the Novelist."

Most of Snow's essays are of passing interest, or of value as they offer hints about his fiction. One deserves a bit more comment. "The Corridors of Power" (1957) —which is also the title for a later novel—expresses succinctly some of Snow's reflections on managers: they are not so different from you or me; the workings of power are better represented by the image of two bureaucrats chatting about a piece of business in the corridor than by lurid images of conspiracy; managers are our best social hope. Part of the significance of the article is that Snow has been one of the few literary men to express any kind of positive approach to the managerial society —he believes that the managerial society is not just a necessary evil but our best hope for the betterment of society.[1]

Before going on to Snow's two major non-fiction writings, we might note in passing Snow's brief encounters with drama. Shortly after he married Pamela Hansford Johnson, he collaborated with her on six conventional one-act plays, one assumes as exercise or *jeu d'esprit*.[2] He has also written a full-length play, *A View over the Park*, which was produced in London in 1950. Here we have the Snow materials and situations: a civil servant hero; conflict within a committee; the combination of motives of self-aggrandizement and public service; the hero's decision that Whitehall would be well lost for love; and the heroine's conviction that for him life without Whitehall would not be worth having. The play was not a success; the reviewer for *The Times* found the members of the commission not men but points of view and said that Snow "had in mind a good play on the theme of political ambition at odds with love, but he has not written it. He has merely put the theme into words." [3] Snow has in effect agreed with the general verdict and has written no more drama.

The most famous and controversial of his non-fiction writings are *The Two Cultures* and *Science and Government*. For anyone who comes to them from the novels their effect is to raise the question of their relation to Snow's fiction. It is clear that they are not of a piece with the novels. There are some common concerns, the interest in power and in science. But one might well imagine the author of the "Strangers and Brothers" sequence to belong to the literary culture scolded in *The Two Cultures*, or one might imagine the author of *The Two Cultures* to be a person without much interest in fiction. Snow put it mildly when he said the novels and the non-fiction are not similar so much as complementary.[4]

There are, one suspects, two sides to Snow. One is the responsible, public-spirited, pragmatic man of affairs. Such qualities are matters of temperament rather than vocation, but, of course, this side is associated with Snow the scientist and administrator. The other side of Snow is the artist. The artist is good at people, finds them interesting in themselves, and forgives their wrong views. He is more concerned with his characters' self-fulfilment than with their social function. Snow as an artist is interested in the workings of society, partly because we should understand how society works, but most fundamentally because it is fascinating. His strongest admiration is for Tolstoy, not the moralist or social theorist, but the man who could bring a scene alive.

These two sides of Snow remain fairly separate. *The Two Cultures* is not graced by the balance, qualification, and fineness of perception of the artist. And the novels are free of the sense of social urgency behind the public utterances.

One suspects that when Snow steps on the lecture platform he appeals to the duality of his own nature as novelist and public man and seeks to reconcile these claims. In *The Two Cultures,* however, the effect is not reconciliation but conflict. Insofar as Snow puts himself forward as a novelist who insists upon the importance of science and technology to help those who do not have enough to eat, he is successful. But the public man speaks harshly of literature as if by way of compensation for being an artist. And it is this that seems to be responsible for many of the difficulties of *The Two Cultures.*

The Two Cultures and the Scientific Revolution was delivered as the Rede Lecture at Cambridge in 1959; it was widely reported and later published. It has continued to be the subject of much discussion since then. Whatever its limitations it has succeeded in at least one of Snow's goals, the stimulation of thought about the problem it raises.

The work—and this is important to note—falls into two fairly distinct parts, which make different though

related points, the first about the scientific and literary
cultures, and the second about the implications of the
scientific revolution. The first half (the sections called
"The Two Cultures" and "Intellectuals as Natural
Luddites") defines the scientific and literary cultures
and illustrates and explores the gap between them. Literary culture is restricted and constrained; scientific culture talks of a new Elizabethan age. Literary culture is
full of *démodé* and anti-social thinking; scientific culture is optimistic about society. Literary culture wishes
the future did not exist; scientific culture has the future
in its bones. Each has a distorted image of the other:
literary culture thinks scientists shallow and unaware of
man's condition; scientific culture thinks literary people
have no foresight, no concern for their fellow men.

In spite of a certain balance in the structure of this
analysis, it is directed, as many critics have pointed out,
against literary culture: literary intellectuals are natural
Luddites; the response of literary culture to the industrial revolution has been a scream of horror.

The second half of *The Two Cultures* (the sections
called "The Scientific Revolution" and "The Rich and
the Poor") shifts to a related but somewhat different
point. It examines the nature of the scientific revolution, and it insists that industrialization is the hope of
the poor and that the advanced countries must assist in
the development of India, Southeast Asia, Africa, Latin
America, the Middle East. But the division in our culture keeps us from taking the vigorous action that is
necessary and urgent. What we must do is to break the
patterns of our education and our thought. We must

understand the importance of science and technology, and we must educate a great many more scientists and technicians than we are now doing.

Snow asserts that the gap between the two cultures is common throughout the West, but clearly his exhortations are to Britain and the United States and as far as details are concerned his diagnosis of the problem and his appeal for change in educational policy are directed chiefly at his fellow countrymen. While the two parts of the talk are related causally—the division between the two cultures is in Snow's view the reason for our failure to meet the challenge of the scientific revolution—the two sections are quite different in tone. The second half presents, in a sober way, a position which is common enough and in its large outlines unexceptionable; the first half is tendentious and has aroused a great deal of controversy.

The reaction, most strikingly Dr. Leavis's denunciation,[5] has been violent. It has been a surprise to Snow, who thought of himself simply as giving a university lecture which would be a minor contribution to an urgent practical problem. The response is also curious in view of the fact that before *The Two Cultures* Snow had made the same points elsewhere. His anonymous article "New Minds for the New World" (*New Statesman*, 1956) made, with a good deal of statistical support, the same kind of plea for a change in the English educational system.[6] And an article entitled "Two Cultures" (also appearing in the *New Statesman* in 1956) is very close to the first section of the Rede Lecture.[7] Yet in neither case was there a strong response, only a few letters, mildly demurring or generally sympathetic.

There are two reasons, I think, for the vigor of the response to *The Two Cultures*. First, the discussion, again in Britain more than in America, is the focus for a much larger social and ethical division: it became instantly in Britain and gradually has become in the United States a party issue. The polemic against literary intellectuals and the proposal to change education, while they have practical ends, in fact touch on much larger attitudes. (For an American the immediate issues just don't seem that momentous.) The subsequent debate has been depressing both in its tone and in its lack of critical intelligence. And much of the debate is concerned not with the problems Snow has raised but with the expression of disapproval or hostility towards people on the other side. Perhaps the violence of many of Snow's attackers supports Snow's rather strong contentions about literary culture's hostility to change.

The second reason for the controversy lies in *The Two Cultures* itself. Its difficulty, I think, is essentially rhetorical.[8] Snow wanted to make some very large and general points and to make them briefly and tellingly. But to do so without over-simplification or without giving offense demanded fineness of judgment, balance, qualification, qualities which Snow the novelist surely has. But the Snow who spoke in *The Two Cultures* was Snow the public man, and the public man, moved by the urgency of the problem, made an unfortunate miscalculation. He did not make qualifications for the sake of precision and did not give sufficient attention to tone. The result is not surprising: the tone has raised unnecessary antagonism and the lack of qualification has left him vulnerable.

A good illustration of the difficulties of tone is the section title "Intellectuals as Natural Luddites": it is a title more suited to polemics than to the essentially sober point of the lecture. In general the difficulties in tone come from the basic miscalculation of mixing two different approaches, that of the novelist scolding and protesting against the reaction of twentieth-century intellectuals, and that of the public man soberly urging action on an important practical problem. Bringing these two together was not happy. Nor was it necessary, for the appeal for action can be made independently of the polemical analysis of the division of our society into two cultures.

The other difficulty is lack of precision, overgeneralization:

> If we forget the scientific culture, then the rest of western intellectuals have never tried, wanted, or been able to understand the industrial revolution, much less accept it.[9]

There is a good deal of truth in this, but for anything as complicated as the history of the last century and a half it is a very considerable over-simplification. The failure is one of rhetoric rather than of knowledge or insight. For the novels and *Science and Government* make clear how aware Snow is of the complexity of such problems. Snow devotes a page or two in *The Two Cultures* to acknowledging the difficulties inherent in the division into two cultures but says he has decided in the

interests of simplicity to retain the dichotomy. Although
Snow's critics have not improved on his analysis, they
are convincing in suggesting that there are more elements in the problem than his formula allows for.

After the initial excitement had time to subside,
Snow returned to the subject with "The Two Cultures:
A Second Look" (1963). The rhetoric is again very
plain, and Snow reminds us that in the earlier lecture he
tried to speak as simply and clearly as possible. He
makes some qualifications, extensions of terms, and dis-
tinctions, and amplifies some points. The major burden
of the essay is to restate his argument in as simple and
unpolemical terms as possible and to bring the discussion forward by reflecting on the response to the piece,
most notably to consider that there may be a third culture, roughly social science, and that that third culture
may hold much hope for bridging the gap. "The Two
Cultures: A Second Look" is a good piece in itself and
good in its tone. It will hardly placate Snow's opponents, but it puts his position on stronger ground.[10]

Science and Government, a series of lectures delivered
at Harvard a year after *The Two Cultures,* is a much
more successful and a more interesting book. Because so
much of it is narrative (fifty out of eighty pages), it
reads easily and with some of the interest of the novels.
Because its aims are more modest, its conclusions and
prescriptions have provoked less controversy than those
of *The Two Cultures.* The full title of the series in
which the lectures were delivered is *"The Godkin Lectures on the Essentials of Free Government and the Du-
ties of the Citizen."* Snow's lectures appropriately offer

some practical observations about how governments work, how decisions get made; he writes out of considerable first-hand experience, not as a cultural historian as in *The Two Cultures.*

We need, says Snow, to understand the relationships of science and government; surprisingly little is known; and the right answers are hard to come by. "The best I can do is tell a story . . . to extract a few generalisations from it, or, to be more sensible, a few working rules." [11]

Snow's story is that of the conflict between two scientists, Tizard and Lindemann, in the shaping of British scientific-military policy in the period 1934–42. The first section characterizes the two men, describes their friendship, and tells of Tizard's struggle to get radar ready in the pre-war years against the opposition of Lindemann. The second section describes Tizard's virtual dismissal as scientific adviser to the Government, the supremacy of Lindemann as scientific overlord, and the controversy during this time about the effectiveness of mass bombing.

The last section of thirty pages is concerned with "empirical prescriptions" and "working tips" to be drawn from the two controversies. Snow gives an interesting analysis of the kinds of closed politics: the classical committee, hierarchic politics, and court politics, all three of them involved in the two controversies. But his chief concern is the meaning of the tale. We can deduce, Snow says, a few ideas of what to avoid—the solitary scientific overlord, and the euphoric scientist carried away by gadgets or secrecy. He lays down several condi-

tions for a good scientific committee—clear and limited
objectives, proper placement within government structure, possession of power of action. In the course of the
discussion Snow expresses his conviction that we need
more scientists in policy-making roles and gives a
thoughtful discussion of the limits of scientists and of
professional administrators.

The peroration of the piece asks, *"Why worry about
science and government?"* [12] We are, says Snow, losing
our sense of the future, living more and more in the
existential moment, we lack a model of the future. Scientists, by their training and the nature of their discipline, are future directed, and they can offer us a kind of
foresight which, for all our wisdom and experience, we
badly lack.

Where *The Two Cultures* created controversy because of its generalizations, *Science and Government* has
created controversy about its account of the character of
Lindemann and about certain events in his career. The
controversy, however, has been limited and restrained.
Although it has been less discussed than *The Two Cultures, Science and Government* has, in its larger implications, been more successful in promoting serious concern with its problem.

In mid-1962 Snow published an *Appendix to Science
and Government,* which is nearly as long as the original
lectures. He gives a "modest grumble" about the complaint that he has treated the Tizard-Lindemann conflict as a novelist would: in his fiction, he says, heroes
and villains are much less distinguishable; and the mel-
odrama of the actual situation is more than a novel

could stand. Snow says that now he might devote more space to the moral than to the story. As for the story, the largest part of the *Appendix* is devoted to the presentation of new material, which greatly strengthens Snow's case. As for the moral, Snow reasserts his belief that, "Whoever he is, whether he is the wisest scientist in the world, we must never tolerate a scientific overlord again." [13]

6 ❧

Snow and His Critics

THE growth of Snow's reputation has been steady and gradual like his growth as a novelist. After the apprentice works a promising novel, then three novels, *Strangers and Brothers*, *The Light and the Dark*, *Time of Hope*, each showing advance and revealing more clearly the nature of Snow's art; with *The Masters*, *The New Men*, and *Homecoming*, the full maturity of the novelist, followed by the steady achievement of the later novels. Criticism has followed a similar pattern: at the beginning Snow is simply a novelist; later a familiar, a promising novelist; a novelist of considerable achievement; a major novelist; and at last an established major

novelist who must be dealt with fully and deferentially.
One could probably plot a curve in terms of the average
length of book reviews (the *Times Literary Supplement*
moving from a perfunctory 600 with *The Light and the
Dark* and a meager 430 with *The Masters* to 2,700 and
1,100 with *Homecoming* and *The Affair*). The length
rises sharply in the mid-nineteen-fifties with *The Masters, The New Men,* and *Homecoming,* and sharply
again after the *Two Cultures* controversy.

Omitting reviews and Pamela Hansford Johnson's
precocious claim in the forties that Snow was "the most
considerable of modern English novelists," [1] criticism
really begins with the fifties. (It is worth recalling that
by 1950 only three of the "Strangers and Brothers" series had been published.) Pamela Hansford Johnson's
essay in the 1950 volume collected by the English Asso-
ciation is a straw in the wind. In "Three Novelists and
the Drawing of Character" she does not go beyond defining Snow as a novelist in whom character is all important, placing him in the tradition of Trollope,
Thackeray, George Eliot, Galsworthy, and Bennett, and
noting that the first three novels of his series contain at
least thirty fully realized and distinct characters, all but
one of whom the author likes.[2] With *The Masters* in
1951 and *The New Men* in 1954 interest in Snow in-
creases. The two novels jointly won the James Tait Black
Memorial Prize of 1954, and *The New Men* was a selection of a highbrow book club for which Lionel Trilling
wrote an essay entitled "The Novel Alive or Dead"; it
isn't dead, he maintains, if it produces a Snow. Trilling's
article, which had much to do with making Snow better

known in the United States, does not find greatness in Snow; it describes him as a plain, modest novelist, businesslike in his way of engaging the emotions and affections. Trilling praises Snow for his sense of social fact, but on the whole reinforces the view of Snow as a twentieth-century Trollope: a man who believes that the novel should give pleasure; who is straightforward as an artist; who operates out of a set of old-fashioned notions, chiefly about loyalty and generosity; who is remarkably tolerant.[3]

The publication of *Homecoming* compelled critics to take Snow more seriously and also began to make clear the design of the "Strangers and Brothers" sequence. An excellent example of this reassessment appears in a 1958 review of *The Conscience of the Rich* by Helen Gardner in the *New Statesman*. Miss Gardner says that until she read *Homecoming* she regarded the series with "lukewarm respect." Snow lacks, she says, "immediacy and imaginative veracity," deficiencies which earlier made her write off the Lewis Eliot novels as being

> no more than intelligent entertainment. But the central chapters of *Homecoming* . . . convinced me that I was wrong. . . . I realised that I had been judging the other novels by a wrong standpoint, had been demanding from the author something inconsistent with what he was giving.

Miss Gardner's point is that Snow is attempting something unique in English, a panoramic novel with a first person narrator, and that the greyness is quite deliberate. Lewis Eliot is indeed "a hero of our time." To "complain of the narrator's priggishness or of the lack of humour with which he views the world is to complain of things which are necessary concomitants of the kind of prolonged and serious self-inquisition which is at the centre of the whole long work." Miss Gardner suggests the unavoidability of comparison with Proust. Though

> the world of Lewis Eliot is a drab one beside that of Marcel . . . [i]t is nonetheless a real fictional world . . . so that we can speak of "a Snow situation" as we speak of "a Proustian experience."

In Snow as in Proust "the ultimate quest is not for success, but for value and meaning." Where Marcel discovers this within himself, Lewis Eliot "is to discover it in the relations of man to men." And where there is a shocking coldness in Proust's masterpiece:

> The appeal of "a Snow situation" is, on the contrary, primarily an appeal to the conscience and to our moral experience. At the heart of the work is the conviction that we are members one of another; and the whole enterprise seems to me the most impressive attempt in our generation to explore through fiction the moral nature of man.[4]

In 1959 Snow achieved a sort of canonization when a volume about him appeared in the British Council series "Writers and their Work." The pamphlet, by Snow's friend the novelist William Cooper, is descriptive rather than evaluative or interpretive. What it suggests more than anything is the sense of Snow as a thoroughly established novelist.

By the beginning of the nineteen-sixties this evaluation had become widespread. Surveys of twentieth-century literature (such as the *Pelican Guide* [1961], Frederick Karl's *Contemporary English Novel* and James Gindin's *Postwar British Fiction* [1962]) began to allot a section to Snow. He became a common point of reference and comparison, and by 1960 it was not surprising to find assertions that Snow is "the one indubitable fictional giant of the English immediate present." [5]

One result of Snow's increasing reputation and of the controversy over *The Two Cultures* is that discussions of Snow's fiction and his ideas have become a field for snobbery and counter-snobbery, for personality mongering, and for attacks on Snow's admirers and detractors.

Snow has not always been fortunate in the quality of the praise he has received. Thus Robert Greacen's "The World of C. P. Snow":

> Snow's message appears to be simply this: it is hard at the moment to see the way ahead, and there will surely be a lot of difficulties and even horrors in front of us, but we must not give up. Difficulties, given intelligence and good will, can be overcome. Science is here to help man, not to destroy him; and science is on the side of optimism. He believes we have several good scientific reasons for taking the long-term view that humanity is indestructible. That is what Snow is saying, in both his fiction and nonfiction, to one reader at least. The world of C. P. Snow has its tragic undertones, to be sure, but its creator believes that in the end humanity will come out on the side of reason and kindness; and that when some of the contempo-

rary tensions can be vitiated, the strangers and enemies of today may well become the brothers and
friends of tomorrow.[6]

This is not even a vulgarization of what Snow is up to;
indeed it sounds rather like one of Snow's characters,
the muddle-headed Herbert Getliffe. Similarly Edmund
Fuller, in a letter to *The New York Times,* associates
Snow with his own dreary set of attitudes toward contemporary literature:

> In a period when the senses dominate fiction, when
> many writers deliberately abdicate reason, he is prom-
> inent among the select group who are artists with
> their minds—not just with their emotions, muscles, or
> glands. At a time when breakdown, despair, and sick-
> ness are pervasive themes, he shows us a large, varied,
> effectively functioning world peopled by all sorts and
> conditions of men. It is an arena of meaningful, pur-
> poseful action in which men are affected by the cha-
> otic elements in their time but need not inevitably be
> engulfed by them.[7]

Among the more real problems that adverse criticism
has raised has been that of defining Snow's kind of art
and of distinguishing the relevant and the irrelevant
virtues and faults. Omitting Leavis's extravagant de-
nunciations ("as a novelist he doesn't exist; he doesn't
begin to exist. He can't be said to know what a novel
is.") [8] and an occasional statement such as Edmund
Wilson's that he finds Snow "almost completely unreadable," [9] unsympathetic critics have generally tended to
give Snow credit for writing about our world, for his
sense of social fact, and for his characterization. But they

find him wanting in other areas. A writer in the *Pelican Guide,* for example, finds the "Strangers and Brothers" series a "remarkable and sustained achievement" but feels that "too often the minutiae of the struggle for power are offered as substitutes for those emotional and imaginative challenges that we expect from great fiction." Snow, he says, has no new technique and his writing is "devoid of anything approaching poetry." [10] Another writer in the same volume makes similar assumptions about the kind of novel Snow is or ought to be writing: "Snow is accurate and painstaking rather than sensitive," he is poor at atmosphere, the private histories "are very thin in their physical and emotional life," the social documentation is good but remains an aggregate because the narrator cannot really unify it.[11]

Rayner Heppenstall in *The Fourfold Tradition* reports himself fascinated by Snow's account of the world of power: the committees are admirably presented. He finds Lewis Eliot a good narrator and says, "I shall listen with care to everything that he tells me, but I do not quite find his mould heroic." [12] And Heppenstall is distressed by the lack of color in Snow's style.

Bernard Bergonzi, complaining in an article in *Twentieth Century* about William Cooper's pamphlet, says that he is trying to put his objections to Snow on a technical plane. Social history is not enough; Snow's prose style is unimpressive and at worst "so arid as to be almost unreadable." Bergonzi's principal objection, however, is to the first person narrator. His presence is too artificial, the novels are too limited by him, and his moral assumptions are "distinctly shallow." And Snow is likely to end up as a period piece like Wells and Bennett.[13]

Attempts to assess Snow's achievement have been plagued by social-political bias, by confusion as to what questions to raise, by uncertainty as to what kind of novel Snow is writing, and by distaste for his kind of novel.

The end of this confusion may be in sight. In the nineteen-sixties, Snow is receiving the treatment standard for established authors. On the one hand he is attacked by those who feel that his reputation is inflated: but on the other hand he is beginning to receive serious and thorough critical scrutiny. He is not yet subject to the exhaustive and tedious specialized study which is routine with an author like Faulkner, but discussions of his work are appearing more and more in the literary journals (there have been articles in *Review of English Literature, Meanjin, Kenyon Review, Critique, Western Humanities Review, Queen's Quarterly,* and a book on Snow issued by a university press). At this point criticism has set itself to the task of defining more precisely the overall themes and structure of the "Strangers and Brothers" sequence and of giving some precision to the description of Snow's art.

If this type of criticism, with its scholarly tendencies, has the characteristic danger of preferring analysis to evaluation, it has strength and timeliness in its willingness to take an author sympathetically on his own terms. The title of an article by Michael Millgate, "Structure and Style in the Novels of C. P. Snow," is suggestive. Making use of Snow's concept of resonance, Millgate indicates how the various themes—possessiveness, love, ambition, spectatorship, strangers and brothers—are played off against each other to structure the "Strangers and Brothers" series. He discusses, with reference to Proust, the structural function of involuntary memory, and he argues that the deliberately cultivated austerity and the insistence on narrative are a means of stripping away inessentials to "present the human situation in naked clarity." [14] Raney Stanford's "Personal Politics in the Novels of C. P. Snow" is concerned not with technique but with the definition of the major theme of the "Strangers and Brothers" sequence, which is in his view the contrast between political-moral abstractions and concern for individuals. Stanford suggests that Snow's opposition to the novel of sensibility is overstated and that his quarrel with it is more one of means than of ends, since personal relations are surely the center of Snow's own work.[15]

Two of the better discussions of Snow's fiction, one American, one English, will give a fair impression of the current status of criticism of Snow. F. R. Karl's chapter on Snow in his *Contemporary English Novel*, though it ignores possessive love and concentrates almost exclusively on power and conscience, gives a thorough analysis of the relation between Snow's method and his large aims. Karl sees Snow as close to the "mature Jane Austen," as a serious novelist concerned with duty and principle rather than as a reporter of social fact. Snow employs social data in order to study the conscience of the good man in a world of ambition and power. The Snow hero must constantly come to terms with himself: con-

science is an almost obsessive notion with Snow. Karl
praises *The Masters* as a study of the workings of power
but finds in *The Affair* a demonstration of the limits of
Snow's belief in reason. Generally, he thinks, Snow is
"weakest when people confront something outside of
themselves, strongest when they must come to terms
with the tortured man within." [16]

Derek Stanford, taking Archilochus' saying, sees Snow
as a fox, who knows many things, unlike a hedgehog
who knows one big thing. He suggests that Snow's use of
clichés and banalities is a deliberate and appropriate instrument for the presentation of reality as it is seen by
"those who have two feet planted on the earth." If
Snow's prose at romantic moments is embarrassingly
bad, it is otherwise right. Similarly the point of view in
the "Strangers and Brothers" series is correctly chosen;
the diffuse and repetitious presentation of events is very
close to our experience of reality; the series is not only a
"naturalistic triumph" but has a "poetry all its own."
Snow's strength is not social analysis, which is inade-
quate, but the analysis of character, in which he goes
deep. And Snow, Stanford thinks, has created a remarkable gallery of portraits. However, Snow's ideas and his
politics get on Stanford's nerves. He feels Snow is weak
at handling ideas and complains about his portrait of
the left and about the "grey progressivism" of Lewis
Eliot. Lewis Eliot's radicalism is, he feels, inconsistent,
for how can he be so hopeful and so radical if he enter-
tains so low a view of human nature. Lewis Eliot's trouble is that he "can neither hope nor hate enough." Stanford suggests that Snow's popularity is symptomatic of

the widespread acceptance of these attitudes at the moment, that British culture is suffering from a "combination of professed radicalism with a comfortable middle-of-the-road" success, that is, from the values of the Left Establishment.[17] (In view of Stanford's disapproval of Snow's political stance, it is curious to note that the hedgehog-fox metaphor which Stanford uses to praise Snow as a novelist has also been used by Arthur M. Schlesinger, Jr., to explain the strength of the American liberal tradition.) [18]

Perhaps the chief problem in evaluating Snow's achievement as a novelist is the inevitable political-cultural involvement of the critic. Lewis Eliot's acceptance of success and his participation in the established order of power in a nearly contemporary world are not things that every reader can take as given. Certainly in Britain many readers find Lewis Eliot—and Snow— complacent, although this has not been so much a problem for American readers, who are removed from the immediate cultural situation, and who seem to have assimilated the conservative and pragmatic quality of Kennedy-Johnson liberalism. Snow's novels involve certain attitudes and ideas, and those ideas are too important to be regarded simply as part of a self-enclosed fictional world. We can avoid the extremes which find Snow either the apostle to the Philistines or the whipping boy of snobs, for these are clearly arguments about ethical stances rather than about Snow's fiction. But we can hardly look at Snow the way we do Dickens. It is too difficult for us to give the writer his subject, for in that choice of subject Snow is not simply constructing an object of contemplation but making judgments about our world.

This difficulty is aggravated by the fact that since Snow speaks simply and without indirection, it is fairly easy to oversimplify and vulgarize what he is trying to do. Thus the assertions that Snow is a writer with a few simple old-fashioned ideas about loyalty and generosity. As some of the political and ethical concerns of Snow's works lose their immediate urgency, and as his art comes to be better defined, we shall, I think, see less of this, and such descriptions of Snow will be in the same class with a description of Jane Austen as a novelist who believed that people should be polite to each other.

Within Snow's fiction itself the chief critical problem is the question of just what kind of novel he is writing. He has perhaps made the problem difficult because in attempting to define and defend his own art he has been unnecessarily hostile to the stream of consciousness novel and the tradition of experiment. This has intensified the complaints that Snow has contributed nothing to the novel and that he is devoid of all resources of art.

The complaint that he has contributed nothing to the novel need not be taken very seriously, but the other objection, that he is without art, points to a genuine problem in assessing Snow's work. The straightforwardness and apparent conventionality of Snow's novels has been a real stumbling block for many readers, and not only for those who have fixed notions of the techniques allowable in fiction. As Helen Gardner has said, it is possible even for a perceptive critic to miss at first the nature of what Snow is attempting. But as the series becomes more widely read and discussed, and as it nears completion, the nature of Snow's art is becoming more generally understood and assessment of his achievement on its own terms is beginning.

A good case of this process appears in the discussions of Snow's style. In the earlier reviews it was repeatedly a source of complaint or at least lament—Trollopian flatness, alkaline flatness, utilitarian newspeak. But of late critics have begun to define the reasons for the plainness of the style, and we now find casual discussions of Snow which refer to the "artfully controlled flatness of Snow's style." [19]

The largest critical problem which still needs attention is that of the narrator. Snow has had to pay a high price for the use of a narrator, but the gains would seem worth the cost. The difficulty that remains is that of distance. Inevitably there cannot be much distance in the portrait of Lewis Eliot, since we must accept all that he tells us as true. Hence certain critics complain that Lewis Eliot's voice is identical with that of Snow and that both are objectionable. A few others see Lewis Eliot as a character who is meant to be judged, and find his limitations quite deliberate. Retrospection of course makes it possible for an older Lewis Eliot to judge a younger one; the pictures of Lewis Eliot's politics in the nineteen-thirties are of this kind. In *The Masters,* there is an effect of distancing, of judgment on Lewis Eliot. As the reader sees the two candidates in the later part of the novel, he is led to feel that Lewis Eliot is over-concerned and that the novel asks us to doubt the soundness of his judgment. In general, however, the reader feels compelled to accept Lewis Eliot's account and has no adequate means for judging him as a character.

As further novels of the "Strangers and Brothers" sequence appear and as it comes to completion, the discussions of Snow will become more intensive and more searching. At this point it is still too early to attempt an exact assessment of Snow's achievement, but it is certainly possible to suggest its general character and the way in which we should look at it.

To suggest a perspective in which we can view Snow, I would like to point to three contemporary ways of looking at power in society—those of Snow, William Golding, and Kingsley Amis. Snow takes the established order of power very seriously: not that he approves of it completely, but that he finds it an important and fascinating subject, worthy of patient and intelligent examination. Golding in *Lord of the Flies* is concerned with the workings of society but on an allegorical level which ignores the world of politics, business, manners, in order to get at the metaphysical relationship between "the defects of society" and "the defects of human nature." [20] Amis sees the subject in terms of satire: "The welfare democracy . . . is a satirical arena far vaster and richer than the stratified democracy which is now yielding place to it." [21] Each of these is clearly a valid way of looking at the world, and the only thing we must be sure of is that we seek from each what it can give us, that we do not demand from one the qualities of the others. This is to say that when we come to evaluate Snow's approach to power or his achievement in general, we have to do so in terms of the realistic tradition in which he is operating.

Among those contemporary writers who have taken a realistic rather than an apocalyptic or satiric view, Snow must, I think, stand first. The tradition of realism has never really died, though in the earlier part of the century it was not employed by any major talent in English. And recently it has shown renewed vitality in novelists like Bacchelli, Sholokhov, Auchincloss, and Cozzens. Snow has the virtues of the realistic tradition—a large and steady view of man and society, which is characterized not so much by brilliant insights as by shrewdness and judgment.

What Snow has got in addition to these qualities—and a large part of what makes him a major novelist—can be seen when we consider what has been the final limitation of much competent and intelligent realism—a certain dullness. Snow is fascinated with whatever is at hand: a piece of business, the motives of a character. And it is this that sets Snow apart from the straightforward realistic novelist with his accurate patient account of things. In some of his statements Snow has spoken of the usefulness of understanding more about power; in his fiction he has created out of this matter a kind of poetry. In his presentation of power, of character, of everything in the world about us, he shows an undulled capacity for wonder.

APPENDIX

References

CHAPTER ONE

1. C. P. Snow, "Author's Note" preceding *The Search,* 1958, p. v ("Note" preceding the American edition of *The Search* differs), and R. W. Saal, "Sir Charles P. Snow," 1960, p. 15. Biographical material on Snow is limited. In addition to the works cited in this chapter, see W. Balliett [Biographical Note], 1955, p. 7; Kunitz and Haycraft, "C. P. Snow," 1955, p. 932; "C. P. Snow," ed. Charles Moritz, 1962, pp. 431 ff.

2. "Chubb Fellow," 1961, p. 44.

3. C. P. Snow, "Note" preceding *The Search,* p. v.

4. *Royal Society Proceedings,* 1930, pp. 355 ff.

5. C. P. Snow, "Science of the Year," 1933, pp. 160–1.

6. S. Gorley Putt, "Technique and Culture: Three Cambridge Portraits," 1961, pp. 18–19.

7. C. P. Snow, "Author's Note" preceding *Death under Sail,* 1959, p. vii.

8. William Cooper, *C. P. Snow,* 1959, p. 9.

9. C. P. Snow, *The Two Cultures,* 1959, p. 1 (2).

10. Pamela Hansford Johnson, "With Prejudice," 1944, p. 5.

11. "Interview with C. P. Snow," 1962, p. 95.

12. William L. Shirer, *The Rise and Fall of the Third Reich,* 1960, p. 784.

13. S. Gorley Putt, *op. cit.,* p. 19.

14. "Interview with C. P. Snow," p. 108.

15. C. P. Snow, "Author's Note" preceding *Death under Sail,* p. vii.

16. C. P. Snow, *The Search,* p. 260 (260).

17. *Op. cit.,* p. 282 (282).

CHAPTER TWO

1. Kenneth Rexroth, "Disengagement: The Art of the Beat Generation," 1957, p. 35.

2. Lionel Trilling, "Manners, Morals, and the Novel," 1950, p. 212.

3. Kingsley Amis, "Laughter's to Be Taken Seriously," 7 Jul. 1957, pp. 1 ff.

4. Bonamy Dobrée, quoted in Derek Stanford, "C. P. Snow: The Novelist as Fox," 1960, p. 251.

5. *H.,* p. 152 (152).

6. *H.,* p. 308 (308).

7. *M.,* p. 346 (336).

8. *N.M.,* p. 300 (300).

CHAPTER THREE

1. R. W. Saal, "Sir Charles P. Snow," 1960, p. 15.

2. William Cooper, *C. P. Snow,* 1959, p. 15.

3. *S. & B.,* p. 45 (37).

4. *S. & B.*, p. 47 (39).

5. *S. & B.*, p. 47 (39).

6. *S. & B.*, p. 291 (280).

7. "Interview with C. P. Snow," pp. 94–5.

8. *L. & D.*, p. 49 (41–2).

9. *L. & D.*, pp. 48–9 (40–1).

10. *L. & D.*, p. 369 (384).

11. *L. & D.*, p. 367 (382).

12. *M.*, pp. 346–7 (336).

13. Earl Lathan, "The Managerialization of the Campus," 1959, pp. 48 ff.

14. *N.M.*, p. 8 (8).

15. *N.M.*, pp. 308–9 (308–9).

16. *N.M.*, p. 215 (215).

17. *N.M.*, p. 86 (85–6).

18. *C.R.*, p. 120 (122).

19. *T.H.*, pp. 115–16 (107–8).

20. *T.H.*, p. 415 (407).

21. *T.H.*, p. 414 (406).

22. "Churchill," in *Look*, 26 Feb. 1963, pp. 29 ff.

23. *M.*, p. 54 (52).

24. *H.*, pp. 249–50 (249–50).

25. *H.*, p. 318 (318).

26. *S. & B.*, p. 309 (298).

27. *N.M.*, p. 301 (301).

CHAPTER FOUR

1. In W. Balliett [Biographical Note], p. 7.

2. C. P. Snow, "The English Realistic Novel," 1957, p. 266.

3. Richard Hoggart, for example, places Snow, along with Amis, Wilson, and L. P. Hartley, in the same tradition as Forster, "The Unsuspected Audience," 1958, pp. 308 ff.

4. C. P. Snow, "Science, Politics, and the Novelist," 1961, pp. 5–6.

5. See "Science, Politics, and the Novelist," and "Interview with C. P. Snow."

6. C. P. Snow, "The Corridors of Power," 1957, p. 620.

7. C. P. Snow, "Science, Politics, and the Novelist," p. 15.

8. C. P. Snow, "The Corridors of Power," p. 619.

9. *L. & D.*, p. 11 (3).

10. *H.*, p. 3 (3).

11. *C.R.*, p. 191 (193).

12. *C.R.*, pp. 85–6 (88).

13. *M.*, pp. 4–5 (4).

14. *M.*, pp. 154–5 (151–2).

15. *H.*, pp. 114–15 (114–15).

16. *N.M.*, p. 135 (135).

17. *N.M.*, pp. 194–5 (194–5).

18. C. P. Snow, "Challenge to the Intellect," 15 Aug. 1958, p. iii.

19. *A.*, pp. 107–8 (97–8).

20. *H.*, p. 188 (188).

21. *N.M.*, p. 155 (155).

22. *N.M.*, p. 39 (39).

23. *M.*, p. 121 (119).

24. *L. & D.*, pp. 131–2 (131).

25. *A.*, p. 250 (246).

26. *A.*, p. 180 (178).

27. See Derek Stanford, "C. P. Snow: The Novelist as Fox," pp. 236 ff.

28. *H.*, p. 400 (400).

29. *H.,* p. 332 (332).

30. *H.,* p. 344 (344).

31. "Challenge to the Intellect," p. iii.

32. *C.R.,* p. vii (American edition omits this "Author's Note").

33. W. Cooper, *C. P. Snow,* p. 33.

34. See *op. cit.,* p. 15.

CHAPTER FIVE

1. C. P. Snow, "The Corridors of Power," p. 619 f.

2. C. P. Snow and Pamela Hansford Johnson, "Spare the Rod," "The Penguin with the Silver Foot," "Her Best Foot Forward," "The Supper Dance," "To Murder Mrs. Mortimer," "Family Party," 1951.

3. "A View over the Park," 31 Aug. 1950, p. 6.

4. "Interview with C. P. Snow," p. 107.

5. F. R. Leavis, "The Significance of C. P. Snow," 1962, pp. 297 ff.

6. C. P. Snow, "New Minds for the New World," 1956, pp. 279 ff.

7. C. P. Snow, "Two Cultures," 1956, pp. 413 ff.

8. See Martin Green, "A Literary Defence of the 'Two Cultures,'" *Critical Quarterly,* 1962, pp. 155 ff. Also in *Kenyon Review,* pp. 731 ff.

9. *Two Cultures,* p. 21 (23).

10. "The Two Cultures: A Second Look," *Times Literary Supplement,* 3, 217, 25 Oct. 1963, pp. 839 ff.

11. *Science and Government,* 1961, pp. 3–4.

12. *Science and Government,* p. 79.

13. *Appendix to Science and Government,* 1962, p. 35.

CHAPTER SIX

1. Quoted in "Johnson, Pamela Hansford," ed. Anna Rothe, 1948, p. 323.

2. Pamela Hansford Johnson, "Three Novelists and the Drawing of Character: C. P. Snow, Joyce Cary and Ivy Compton-Burnett," 1950, pp. 82 ff.

3. Lionel Trilling, "The Novel Alive or Dead," pp. 125 ff.

4. Helen Gardner, "The World of C. P. Snow," 1958, pp. 409–10.

5. Charles Brady, "The British Novel Today," 1959–60, p. 530.

6. Robert Greacen, "The World of C. P. Snow," 1961, p. 274.

7. Edmund Fuller, 22 Apr. 1962, p. 25.

8. F. R. Leavis, "The Significance of C. P. Snow," p. 298.

9. Edmund Wilson, "An Interview with Edmund Wilson," 2 June 1962, p. 118.

10. Gilbert Phelps, "The Novel Today," 1961, p. 482.

11. Graham Martin, "Novelists of Three Decades: Evelyn Waugh, Graham Greene, C. P. Snow," 1961, pp. 410, 412.

12. Rayner Heppenstall, *The Fourfold Tradition*, 1961, p. 234.

13. Bernard Bergonzi, "The World of Lewis Eliot," 1960, pp. 215, 224. See Peter Fison's "Reply to Bernard Bergonzi's 'The World of Lewis Eliot,' " pp. 568 f.

14. Michael Millgate, "Structure and Style in the Novels of C. P. Snow," 1958, p. 41.

15. Raney Stanford, "Personal Politics in the Novels of C. P. Snow," 1958, pp. 16 ff.

16. Frederick Karl, *The Contemporary English Novel*, 1962,

ই References

p. 84, pp. 82–3. See also his *The Politics of Vision: The Novels of C. P. Snow,* 1963.

17. Derek Stanford, "C. P. Snow: The Novelist as Fox," pp. 237, 244, 244, 246.

18. Arthur M. Schlesinger, Jr., "The One Against the Many," 14 Jul. 1960, pp. 9 ff.

19. Charles Brady, "The British Novel Today," p. 539.

20. William Golding, quoted in "Notes" following *Lord of the Flies,* 1955, p. 250.

21. Kingsley Amis, "Laughter's to Be Taken Seriously," p. 1.

Bibliography

NOTE

The Search and the novels in the "Strangers and Brothers" sequence are now available in uniform editions, published by Macmillan in England and Scribners in the United States. The date of the first English publication is given when it differs from that of the standard edition. Editions marked with an asterisk are taken as standard.

1. C. P. SNOW

FICTION

Death under Sail. London (Heinemann) 1932. (Revised and reissued) * 1959.

New Lives for Old. London (Gollancz) 1933.

The Search. London (Gollancz) 1934. (Revised edn.) (Macmillan) * 1958. New York (Scribners) (revised edn.) * 1959. (The English and American revised editions have different prefatory notes.)

Strangers and Brothers. London (Faber) 1940 (Macmillan) * 1958. New York (Scribners) * 1960.

[154]

ᢒᣞ Bibliography

The Light and the Dark. London (Faber) 1947 (Macmillan) *
1952. New York (Scribners) * 1961.

Time of Hope. London (Faber) 1949 (Macmillan) * 1950. New
York (Scribners) * 1961.

The Masters. London (Macmillan) 1951, * 1952. New York
(Scribners) * 1960.

The New Men. London (Macmillan) 1954, * 1957. New York
(Scribners) * 1955.

Homecomings (in U.S. *Homecoming*). London (Macmillan) *
1956. New York (Scribners) * 1956.

The Conscience of the Rich. London (Macmillan) * 1958. New
York (Scribners) * 1958. (U.S. edition omits important "Author's Note.")

The Affair. London (Macmillan) * 1960. New York (Scribners) *
1960.

Corridors of Power. London (Macmillan) * 1964. New York
(Scribners) * 1964.

OTHER WRITINGS

(Together with E. K. Rideal) "Infra-red Investigations of Molecular Structure—Part IV. The Overtone of Nitric Oxide," in
Royal Society Proceedings, 126 (1930), pp. 355 ff.

"Science of the Year," in *Bookman* (London), LXXXV (1933), pp.
159 ff.

"Rejuvenation Promises an End of Old Age," in *Pictorial Review*, 35 (May 1934), pp. 4 ff.

"Enjoyment of Science," in *Spectator*, 156 (1936), pp. 1074 f.

"False Alarm in Physics," in *Spectator*, 157 (1936), pp. 628 f.

"What We Need from Applied Science," in *Spectator*, 157 (1936),
p. 904.

"Superfluity of Particles," in *Spectator*, 157 (1936), pp. 984 f.

"Humanity of Science," in *Spectator*, 158 (1937), pp. 702 f.

"Controlling Reproduction," in *Spectator*, 159 (1937), pp. 678 f.

Richard Aldington, An Appreciation, London (W. Heinemann)
1938.

"Careers," in *Political Quarterly,* 15 (1944), pp. 310 ff.

"The Wisdom of Niels Bohr," in *The Saturday Book,* ed. Leonard Russell, London (Hutchinson) 1949, pp. 180 ff.

"Books and Writers," in *Spectator,* 185 (1950), p. 320.

(Together with Pamela Hansford Johnson) "Spare the Rod," "The Penguin with the Silver Foot," "Her Best Foot Forward," "The Supper Dance," "To Murder Mrs. Mortimer," "The Family Party" (all one-act plays), London (Evans Bros.) 1951.

"Reflections on Mr. Dean's Report," in *Spectator,* 192 (1954), pp. 283 f.

"Storytellers for the Atomic Age," in *New York Times Book Review,* 30 Jan. 1955, pp. 1 ff.

"New Minds for the New World," in *New Statesman and Nation,* LII (1956), pp. 279 ff. (Published anonymously but identified in *The Two Cultures* and *Science and Government.*)

"Two Cultures," in *New Statesman and Nation,* LII (1956), pp. 413 f.

"Irregular Right," in *Nation,* 182 (1956), pp. 238 f.

"The English Realistic Novel," in *Moderna Sprak,* LI (1957), pp. 265 ff.

"The Corridors of Power," in *The Listener,* LVII (1957), pp. 619 f.

"Men of Fission," in *Holiday,* 23 (Apr. 1958), pp. 94 ff.

"Future of Man," in *Nation,* 187 (1958), pp. 124 f.

"Changing Nature of Love," in *Mademoiselle,* XXXXVI (1958), pp. 105 ff.

"Challenge to the Intellect," in *Times Literary Supplement,* 2949, 15 Aug. 1958, p. iii.

The Two Cultures and the Scientific Revolution, Cambridge (Cambridge University Press) * 1959. New York (Cambridge University Press) * 1959.

"The 'Two-Cultures' Controversy, Afterthoughts," in *Encounter,* XIV (Feb. 1960), pp. 64 ff.

&~ Bibliography

"Science, Politics, and the Novelist," in *Kenyon Review*, XXIII (1961), pp. 1 ff.

"Moral Un-neutrality of Science," in *Science*, CXXXIII (1961), pp. 256 ff.

Science and Government, Cambridge, Mass. (Harvard University Press) 1961.

"On Magnanimity," in *Harpers*, 225 (Jul. 1962), pp. 37 ff.

"Interview with C. P. Snow," in *A Review of English Literature*, III (1962), pp. 91 ff.

Appendix to Science and Government, Cambridge, Mass. (Harvard University Press) 1962.

"Churchill," in *Look*, 26 Feb. 1963, pp. 29 ff.

"The Two Cultures: A Second Look," in *Times Literary Supplement*, 3, 217, 25 Oct. 1963, pp. 839 ff.

2. OTHERS

ALLEN, WALTER: *Tradition and Dream*, London 1964.

AMIS, KINGSLEY: "Laughter's to Be Taken Seriously," in *New York Times Book Review*, 7 Jul. 1957, pp. 1 ff.

BALLIETT, W.: [Biographical Note] in *Saturday Review*, 38, 8 Jan. 1955, p. 7.

BERGONZI, BERNARD: "The World of Lewis Eliot," in *Twentieth Century*, 167 (1960), pp. 214 ff.

BRADY, CHARLES A.: "The British Novel Today," in *Thought*, XXX (Winter 1959–60), pp. 518 ff.

"Chubb Fellow," in *The New Yorker*, XXXVII, 16 Dec. 1961, pp. 44 ff.

COOPER, WILLIAM: *C. P. Snow*, London and New York 1959.

FISON, PETER: "A Reply to Bernard Bergonzi's 'World of Lewis Eliot,'" in *Twentieth Century*, 167 (1960), pp. 568 f.

FULLER, EDMUND: "Snow-Leavis Affair," in *New York Times Book Review*, 22 Apr. 1962, pp. 24 f.

GARDNER, HELEN: "The World of C. P. Snow," in *New Statesman*, 55 (1958), pp. 409 f.

GINDIN, JAMES: *Postwar British Fiction*, Berkeley 1962.

GOLDING, WILLIAM: *Lord of the Flies*, New York 1959.

GREACEN, ROBERT: "The World of C. P. Snow," in *Texas Quarterly*, IV (1961), pp. 266 ff.

——: *The World of C. P. Snow*, London 1963.

GREEN, MARTIN: "A Literary Defence of the 'Two Cultures,' " in *Critical Quarterly*, IV (1962), pp. 155 ff., and in *Kenyon Review*, XXIV (1962), pp. 731 ff.

HAMILTON, KENNETH: "C. P. Snow and Political Man," in *Queen's Quarterly*, LXIX (1962), pp. 416 ff.

HEPPENSTALL, RAYNER: *The Fourfold Tradition*, New York 1961.

HOGGART, RICHARD: "The Unsuspected Audience," in *New Statesman*, 56 (1958), pp. 308 ff.

"Johnson, Pamela Hansford," in *Current Biography 1948*, ed. Anna Rothe, New York 1949, pp. 322 f.

JOHNSON, PAMELA HANSFORD: "Three Novelists and the Drawing of Character: C. P. Snow, Joyce Cary and Ivy Compton-Burnett," in *Essays and Studies 1950*, London 1950, pp. 82 ff.

——: "With Prejudice," in *The Windmill*, No. 1 (1944), pp. 1 ff.

KARL, FREDERICK: *The Contemporary English Novel*, New York 1962.

——: *The Politics of Vision: The Novels of C. P. Snow*, Carbondale 1963.

KAZIN, ALFRED: "A Gifted Boy from the Midlands," in *Reporter*, XX, 5 Feb. 1959, pp. 37 ff.

KERMODE, FRANK: *Puzzles and Epiphanies*, New York 1962.

KUNITZ, STANLEY J. and HOWARD HAYCRAFT: "C. P. Snow," in *Twentieth Century Authors, First Supplement*, New York 1955, p. 932.

LATHAN, EARL: "The Managerialization of the Campus," in *Public Administration Review*, XIX (1959), pp. 48 ff.

LEAVIS, F. R.: "The Significance of C. P. Snow," in *Spectator*, 9 Mar. 1962, pp. 297 ff.

⁊❧ Bibliography

———: *The Two Cultures: The Significance of C. P. Snow*, London and New York 1963.

MANDEL, E. W.: "C. P. Snow's Fantasy of Politics," in *Queen's Quarterly*, LXIX (1962), pp. 24 ff.

MARTIN, GRAHAM: "Novelists of Three Decades: Evelyn Waugh, Graham Greene, C. P. Snow," in *The Modern Age* (Pelican Guide to English Literature), Harmondsworth and Baltimore 1961, pp. 394 ff.

MILLGATE, MICHAEL: "Structure and Style in the Novels of C. P. Snow," in *A Review of English Literature*, 1 (Apr. 1960), pp. 34 ff.

PHELPS, GILBERT: "The Novel Today," in *The Modern Age* (Pelican Guide to English Literature) Harmondsworth and Baltimore 1961, pp. 473 ff.

PUTT, S. GORLEY: "Technique and Culture: Three Cambridge Portraits," in *Essays and Studies 1961*, London 1961, pp. 17 ff.

REXROTH, KENNETH: "Disengagement: The Art of the Beat Generation," in *New World Writing*, 11, New York 1957, pp. 28 ff.

ROBBINS, RICHARD: "The Bowles Affair," in *New Republic*, 9 Oct. 1961, pp. 19 ff. (Parody.)

SAAL, R. W.: "Sir Charles P. Snow," in *Saturday Review*, XXXXIII, 7 May 1960, p. 15.

SCHLESINGER, ARTHUR M., JR.: "The One Against the Many," in *Saturday Review*, XLV, 14 Jul. 1962, pp. 9 ff.

SHIRER, WILLIAM L.: *The Rise and Fall of the Third Reich*, New York 1960.

"Snow, C. P.," in *Current Biography Yearbook 1961*, ed. Charles Moritz, New York 1962, pp. 431 ff.

STANFORD, DEREK: "C. P. Snow: The Novelist as Fox," in *Meanjin*, XIX (1960), pp. 236 ff.

STANFORD, RANEY: "Personal Politics in the Novels of C. P. Snow," in *Critique*, II (1958), pp. 16 ff.

———: "The Achievement of C. P. Snow," in *Western Humanities Review*, XVI (1962), pp. 43 ff.

THALE, JEROME: "C. P. Snow: The Art of Worldliness," in *Kenyon Review,* XXII (1960), pp. 621 ff.

TRILLING, LIONEL: "Manners, Morals, and the Novel," in *The Liberal Imagination,* New York 1950, pp. 205 ff.

——: "The Novel Alive or Dead," in *A Gathering of Fugitives,* New York 1956, pp. 125 ff.

——: "Science, Literature & Culture, A Comment on the Leavis-Snow Controversy," in *Commentary,* 33 (1962), pp. 461 ff.

"View over the Park," in *The Times,* 31 Aug. 1950, p. 6.

WILSON, EDMUND: "An Interview with Edmund Wilson," in *The New Yorker,* 38 (2 June 1962), pp. 118 ff.

78562